W9-AEA-444

THE
PRAISE OF FOLLY
AND OTHER PAPERS

BY

BLISS PERRY

Author of " Park-Street Papers," " A Study of Poetry '
" The American Mind," etc.

TOVT BIEN OV RIEN

The Riverside Press

BOSTON AND NEW YORK
HOUGHTON MIFFLIN COMPANY
The Riverside Press Cambridge
1923

The Riverside Press
CAMBRIDGE · MASSACHUSETTS
PRINTED IN THE U.S.A.

TO
G. P.

PREFACE

In which the Author presents his Excuses, Hat in Hand

MOST of these papers have already been printed. "But why, then, publish?" as Pope once remarked. I fear that I cannot answer that searching question very satisfactorily. My previous collections of essays have been kindly received, but I cannot pretend that the welcome was embarrassingly uproarious. Perhaps I like the quieter reception better, not being used to the other kind. At any rate, I am grateful for the courteous permission of the editors of the "Yale Review," the "Century," the "Nation," the "Harvard Graduates' Magazine," and the "Proceedings of the American Academy of Arts and Letters," to allow me to reprint some of the biographical and critical essays contained in this volume. Many of them, like the title essay, "The Praise of Folly," the Harvard Phi Beta Kappa address on "Poetry and Politics," and the study of "Literary Criticism in American Periodicals" — originally delivered as the Bromley Lectures at Yale in 1914 — were written primarily for academic public occasions, and I do not doubt that they betray here and there some traces of that homiletic over-emphasis which characterized my teaching and preaching ancestors.

I admit that this is a sin, though perhaps it is not one of the seven deadliest. A friendly critic of my book on Walt Whitman, many years ago, asserted that when I first wandered away from my native New England, I was careful to paste the Ten Commandments in the top of my hat. I have long since lost that hat, and cannot prove that the critic was mistaken. But I will not deny that I have retained from inheritance and early associations a respect for standards, and I am aware that readers who rebel against all standards will dislike certain pages of this book. Well, "If they like anything," said Thackeray, "one ought to be satisfied." But suppose they do not like anything in the volume? In that case I shall be sincerely sorry, and my grief will be shared by the publishers, but it is now too late for true repentance and amendment of my ways. All that I can do is secretly to begin to believe my friend's story, and to put all the blame for my dogmatism upon that Hat.

B. P.

CONTENTS

THE PRAISE OF FOLLY

I

I SHALL begin, like the old-fashioned novelist,
with a solitary horseman. He is riding from Italy
toward England, a little more than four hundred
years ago. I cannot describe the horse, although
it may have been that very palfrey which our
traveler once borrowed from an English host, and
liked so well that he forgot to return it. But it is
easy enough to describe the rider, for his friend
Holbein has drawn that face lovingly more than
once.

It is a thin, clear face, with a wide brow, keen
blue eyes, delicate nostrils, and a mouth, if anything, too finely cut; a mobile face, half church-
man's, half courtier's, with the aspect of a scholar,
a skeptic, and a gentleman. He has turned forty,
and he has never been robust. Yet he has gone
far, in spite of his frail body and the bar sinister
upon his birth, and he is destined to go farther
still. He has been the companion of princes and
prelates. It is the great Pope Julius II who has
allowed him to wear that costume, half cleric, half
lay; and he is now riding to the court of the young
King Henry VIII of England, dreaming, like

many another humanist, that the golden age of tolerance and learning is at last at hand.

He rides with a loose rein, one may fancy, as did John Wesley long afterward, that he may the more easily read and write as he journeys. One bright day he pulls out his tablets with a happy smile; he has thought of a new pun; yes, by Hercules and all the saints, a pun that will make a good title for a new book. For he has been thinking of his best friend in England, a young lawyer of London, a devout Catholic, a Humanist and Platonist like himself, a gentle spirit who loved children and pet animals and the antics of his professional fool; a dreamer, too, an idealist who in another score of years will be Lord Chancellor, and then a martyr and saint — canonized not only by his Church, but by all who love a white-souled courage — Thomas More. The horseman chuckles to himself as he remembers that that name More, if written in the Latin which both men habitually spoke, becomes Morus, that is to say, "fool." What an odd name for the cleverest man in England! And is not Thomas More's real charm — as his friend thinks — in his innocence of soul, his unworldliness, the happy folly of an unspoiled nature? The Greeks had a name for that, Moria. Why not amuse one's self on the journey, and one's friends by and by, with

480
230
536
260

1306

composing a panegyric upon foolishness, which
shall also be an encomium of More himself? And
so the horseman scribbles triumphantly his pun-
ning title: "Encomium Moriæ." For the book is
to be none other than the famous "Praise of
Folly"; and I hope that — quite as in the old-
fashioned novel — you will already have guessed
the name of the solitary horseman. It is Erasmus;
Desiderius Erasmus of Rotterdam.

The gay little book was finished in London,
under More's own roof, and was published in
1512, four years earlier than More's "Utopia."
Like the "Utopia," it is written in Latin, for the
eyes of cultivated Europe, and for people who can
take a joke. You may read it to-day in more than
one delightful English version, adorned with the
quaint woodcuts of Holbein. There you will see
Folly — who is, by the way, a young woman —
setting up her pulpit in the streets and preaching
to all comers. She "cries aloud," as Wisdom did
of old, but she does not shriek or threaten. She
merely declaims, with infinite merriment and
zest, the praise of foolishness, and by foolishness
she means not merely a happy heedlessness, an
obedience to impulse, a girlish spontaneity and
trustfulness of the world; she means also innocence, purity of soul, that divine "foolishness of
God" which is wiser than men. Yet, like so many

idealists of the Renaissance, our street preacher is also a satirist. She cracks her light whip around the ears of selfishness and stupidity and vice. She has her laugh at pedantry. She pricks the swollen ambition of churchmen. She hates cruelty. She flames out against the selfish wars of kings. And, by contrast, she loves a born simpleton — a half-witted court fool, for instance, because in all his "silliness" there is a true "blessedness." Such a one is nearer to God than any worshiper of images, any seller of indulgences, any conceited school-master, any philosopher at whom Nature is laughing. Folly has a scorn for all pretenders, all princes who are foes of learning, liberty, and justice, all Popes and Cardinals who have forgotten the rude fisherman of Galilee. She invents a passage about pretense running through all society which might have been written by Thackeray, and her description of a Prince as a player with borrowed robes must have been coveted by Carlyle for "Sartor Resartus."

But Folly explains at the last that her "small declamation" is really not a satire, but a panegyric. She is merely, she says, following the example of Ecclesiastes the Preacher, and the example of Saint Paul himself. For did not Paul say, "I speak as a fool," knowing it to be the peculiar privilege of fools to speak the truth without giving offense? Did he not assert that "it pleased God by foolishness to save the world," implying that by wisdom it could never have been saved? Did not our Lord himself say, "Woe unto you, scribes and Pharisees" — that is, woe unto you wise men — whereas He seemed chiefly delighted with children, women, and illiterate fishermen? And the merry speaker closes gravely, in a passage wherein the teaching of Saint Paul is strangely mingled with the doctrines of Neo-Platonism, by pointing out that the Christian religion seems a kind of alliance with Folly; that boys, old women, and fools are nearest the altar; that the true wisdom is to be wholly ravished with things eternal and invisible; and whether one so ravished be in the body or out of the body, who shall say?

I cannot hope, in such a brief summary as I have here attempted, to convey the charm of this playful and subtle book. But the drift of it is perhaps clear enough. At once an imaginary declamation, an encomium upon Thomas More, a satire without bitterness, a medley of Classicism and Christianity, of reverence and irreverence, of nonsense and truth, it is really a Praise of Innocence, an extravaganza composed upon the Beatitude, "Blessed are the pure in heart."

You will note two distinctions which Erasmus

is careful to make. It is true that he praises the simplicity of ignorance, that his own sympathy lies not with the scribes and Pharisees, but with the fishermen of the Galilean Lake. Yet he is himself a most accomplished scribe, an intellectual aristocrat. It is clear, then, that he finds no virtue in ignorance itself, but only in that innocence of spirit which may be found in a Thomas More as well as in a clown. The Renaissance zest for knowledge, that zest which Rabelais compares to a fire sweeping through dry branches, was unabated in Erasmus to the end. It survived every disillusion. His "Praise of Folly" is not a document of reaction; it is rather a hymn to "the breath and finer spirit of all knowledge," the secret which is hidden from the eyes of pedantry and pride.

More subtle still is his attack upon worldliness. The Renaissance was an epoch when worldliness sat high in the saddle and rode mankind; and Erasmus was a man of his age. From boyhood a favorite companion of the great, he is addressing his praise of unworldliness to the future Lord Chancellor of England. What, then, does he mean? That one should avoid the world, like those wearers of black and gray and white gowns whom Erasmus distrusted and despised? Surely not! The unworldliness which he praises is the freedom from spiritual entanglement, the clear-

6

sighted sense of relative values, the ability to keep one's self unspotted by the world even while one is playing a great rôle in the world. Thirty years later, in those sad final days at Basle, Erasmus must have remembered his "Encomium Moriæ" when the news came from England that Sir Thomas More had laid down the Chancellorship and walked serenely to the scaffold, in loyalty to a mere theory of the supreme jurisdiction of the Papacy. More's act was ill advised, says a modern specialist, Sir Sidney Lee; it was obscurantism. Erasmus had a simpler name for it. Himself incapable, perhaps, of such a supreme act of will, he would have called More's voluntary death a sublime folly which the world can neither give nor take away — one of those splendid foolish things which confound the wise.

II

PERHAPS my readers may agree with me in thinking that the "Encomium Moriæ" is an interesting old book, without agreeing in the least that it has some pertinent suggestions for American college men and college women. Yet it seems to me that the little lady imagined by Erasmus hints to her modern brothers and sisters in cap and gown that their wisdom will not be the truest wisdom until it is blended with what Plato

7

and Saint Paul and Erasmus called "foolishness."
Knowledge may be had in any of our knowledge-
shops if you have time and money for such shop-
ping. But Wisdom tarries, like some late-flower-
ing shrub. She has always tarried. There is no
gardener's trick that can force the human plant
to flower into wisdom until the right day dawns.

If the Renaissance lady in cap and bells could
see the life of our American universities, she
would find, no doubt, a variety of delightful ob-
servations to make and of things to praise. Yet I
think she would discover two or three faults in
us: our spirit of knowingness, our spirit of calculation, and our spirit of fear.

Take, first, our knowingness. Every one is
aware that within the lifetime of middle-aged
persons the field of human knowledge has been
indefinitely extended and subdivided. A mass
of new facts, of new generalizations, of hitherto
unsuspected relations, has been revealed by
science. The contemporary mind staggers under
the weight of this new material. We cannot as yet
assimilate it, cannot transmute it into wisdom.
Yet we must recognize its existence, must act as
if we really possessed it and had always possessed
it — precisely as the newly rich hasten to adapt
their habits to an increased income. All around
us, in the professions, in the economic and social

8

life of the community, you will find this new half-knowledge. It is a half-knowledge which has not had time to grow modest, to become aware of its deficiencies. It pretends for the moment to be knowledge, but it is not; it is only knowingness. The real pioneers of science are modest men, but we, the camp-followers who sit around the camp-fires and read the newspapers, are braggarts and sciolists. This is one of the temptations of our facile adaptable American temperament. We cannot help putting most of our goods into the shop window. And if the American father is forced to do this in his business and the American mother is tempted to do it in her club, how are their sons and daughters to escape the same tendency?

Most college students of the present day have had wide opportunity to see something of the world. They are sophisticated. Now a sophisticated person is not one who knows too much — for nobody can possibly, in this short life, ever know enough. The sophisticated person is one who knows too much of some things and too little about other things; he is the very pattern of that "knowingness" which mistakes half-knowledge for the truth. When Mr. Kipling, many years ago, published his "Light that Failed," Mr. Barrie, then a young journalist, made this shrewd

9

comment upon Dick Heldar, Mr. Kipling's hero:
"This man is under the curse of thinking that he
knows everything. He believes that because he
has knocked about the world in shady company
he has no more to learn. It never dawns upon him
that he is but a beginner in knowledge of life compared to many men who have stayed at home
with their mothers." I do not know more exact
phrases than Mr. Barrie's in which to describe
the spirit of the plays and novels from which many
undergraduates are now getting their notions of
what they call "real life." The stage and the
stories present specialized phases of that sophisticated knowingness which is one of the penalties
of our contemporary civilization. They afford a
cheap initiation into certain abnormalities of
artificial society, but their cleverness cannot
conceal their ignorance of normal human life,
and their willful misunderstanding of its scale of
values. The "Colloquies" of Erasmus show us a
man who had himself seen a good deal of shady
company as he rode up and down the Europe of
his day, but this free-spoken man of the Renaissance represents rosy-cheeked innocence when
compared to the brisk knowingness of such undergraduate favorites as the plays of Mr. Shaw, the
novels of Mr. Wells, and the autobiography of
Mr. George Moore.

There is another form of knowingness for which our classrooms are directly responsible. We teachers, in our social and ethical enthusiasms, are constantly delivering ourselves of immature and amateur judgments upon the most complicated problems of the day. The sociology and the politics of the popular pulpit are queer enough, but I suspect that our *obiter dicta* of the classroom are queerer still. Whatever we are supposed to be teaching, we are subconsciously endeavoring to train our pupils for citizenship in a democracy. As ethical instinct this is admirable, but too often we do not really train our pupils; we only excite them with our own eager chatter. We talk knowingly when we do not really know; that is our academic sin.

I have said that the little lady in cap and bells would find a second fault with our college world, namely, its spirit of studied calculation. Like our sad or smug knowingness, this spirit, too, has stolen into the college world from contemporary forces outside the college. It betrays a lack of faith in instinct, in spontaneity. We have too much university machinery in proportion to the power plant; too much organization for the size of the organs which are to be organized. We offer courses in the theory of efficiency, but the efficient person is as rare as ever. Emerson complained humorously in his Journal in the 1840's that in the New England of that day there was "too much comment on the movement by the mover." What would he have thought of some of our recent American performances, where the mover is identical with the movement? This restless self-seeking has attacked our academic life in every stage from the preparatory school to the graduate school. It disguises itself as public service to the academic community, but the way to that service lies, it is thought, through recognized leadership, through office-holding; and here enters the spirit of calculation, of regard for the tangible prizes of academic life. Boys in preparatory schools know perfectly well who the "big" men are in the colleges of their choice; they are the men who have "made" this or that team or club or organization, and they propose to do likewise. They plan their work and calculate their very friendships with these tangible rewards in view.

Undoubtedly the honors paid to-day to the young men who have "done" things, or "made" things, serve to develop some useful practical qualities. But these are for the most part worldly qualities, prematurely vocational, shrewdly materialistic, and hostile to the true simplicity and spontaneity of youth. If I could cut one word out

12

of the current academic vocabulary, it would be the word "prominent." I cannot help wondering what the witty Erasmus of Rotterdam would say if he could see in our American newspapers photographs of "prominent" undergraduate athletes, "prominent" undergraduate office-holders, "prominent" Christians, and even "prominent" Freshmen.

"As we grow older," said Sainte-Beuve, "we grow hard in some spots, and we grow soft in others, but we do not grow ripe." Out of this hardness and softness of half-knowledge, we conjure up strange fears. That spontaneous trust in Nature which marked the Renaissance has given place to forebodings. We are assured that the sun is growing cold, that the supply of fuel is limited, that the fertility of the soil is diminishing, that the race is deteriorating.

This "new fear," as a novelist has lately called it, arises in part from the abnormal attention directed to the future by the rapid progress of science and invention. The new knowledge confers upon man, only too evidently, enhanced destructive powers. We have made terrible tools already, and more are in the making, and we begin to suspect that men cannot be trusted with them. The dread of man thus grows with the dread of the very machinery which man has created. At this moment and in this country good men are perpetuating and popularizing and capitalizing a theory of international fear.

Now, as between this new sophisticated fear of Nature and of man, and the sixteenth century's naïve faith in Nature and man, which is the truer wisdom? Their world was in many ways a far worse world than ours; but they had higher spirits than we, and a more robust laughter. Erasmus and his friends were our equals, if not our superiors, in intellect, in knowledge of men and women, in true efficiency. But they kept their delicacy of touch, their sense of humor, their essential innocence, their childlike faith in Nature. That old Humanism of theirs had its weaknesses, no doubt, but it can still teach us many things: an unashamed fear of God, a bright confidence in the goodness of his world, an innocent simplicity of soul.

If the scholar who wrote "The Praise of Folly" four hundred years ago were talking to us, would he not still say: "'Tis a brave world, my young masters and bachelors and doctors! Do not be afraid of it. Do not calculate your chances so closely that you miss your chance. Do not pretend to know what you do not know. Work and laugh and give thanks, for these three are one. You did not make the world. You cannot remake it. You cannot even spoil it. You may, indeed, have the felicity of improving some little corner of it, but in general the world has been pronounced 'very good.' Enter into its joy."

THE WRITTEN WORD [1]

THE distinction between the written word and the spoken or pictured word seems temptingly easy. Give a man an idea, and can he not shout it aloud, write it in a letter, draw it in a cartoon? Sometimes, assuredly, he can. Take, for instance, the conception "Boss Tweed is a thief." Tilden said it, Godkin wrote it, Nast drew it. These three masters of various modes of expression succeeded in conveying approximately the same idea to the ear, the eye, the brain of the people of New York.

Approximately, no doubt; but yet not precisely the same idea to any two persons. Here we touch, at the very outset, upon the fundamental mystery of all these modes of human intercourse, namely, their symbolic character. The earliest known writing does not attempt to convey the words of a spoken language. It makes signs — rough cartoons, we may call them — which denote concrete objects. It can picture "Fat-Man-Who-Steals" long before it can spell and write the abstract word "thief." If we linger over the mystery of these primitive signs for things, and

[1] Read at the Convocation of the University of the State of New York, 1916.

their gradual change into signs for sounds, we shall never have done, even if we do not attempt to penetrate the deeper mystery of how certain speech-sounds came to be signs of emotions, of facts, of ideas. No one knows what ages of human effort are necessary before one two-legged individual can say or write to another, "Boss Tweed is a thief," and be sure that he is understood.

Our cardinal fact is that by means of these arbitrary speech-sounds, however developed, and the no less arbitrary written and printed signs for speech-sounds, however perfected, human thought and feeling is communicable. The behavior of spoken and written words is full of strange matters, but underneath the fascinating question of behavior is this primary function of communicating the experience of one to the body and mind of another, and so on and on, in wider and wider circles, until we reach the end — what end who knows? Many a reader who cannot accept Tolstoy's theory of art in its entirety has been profoundly impressed with Tolstoy's belief that the sharable quality of art, its capacity for bringing men into spiritual union with one another, is its most significant feature. Certainly the development of primitive literatures, as far as we can trace them, gives constant evidence of the presence of this communal emotion, this function of art as social consolidation. The bodily and mental excitement of the exceptional "creative" individual soon affects the surrounding crowd, as may be seen in the chorus of a sailor's chanty or of a cowboy ballad. The infection of the crowd instantly reacts upon the individual. All primitive, communal literature, like the Hebrew lyric, the Scotch ballad, bears this mark of the body. "My heart and my flesh cry out for the living God": that is a test of genuineness and greatness. The "body-and-mind" experiences of an individual or a group, thus communicated, perpetuate themselves. A few of them get transferred to clay cylinders or papyrus or stone or bronze; and thus the visual and tactile imagination of one man, of one tribe, become, through the mediation of written speech, a part of the spiritual possessions, the "body-and-mind" reactions of civilizations yet unborn.

Now this process continues without cessation. The latest Imagist poet is in this respect, if in no other, like King David or Sappho. He transfers his mental images — which are often, it is true, so purely retinal as scarcely to deserve the name of mental — into written signs for sounds. He thus exposes his body to the world, or to that limited portion of the world which reads his verses. The art of printing gives him a chance — indeed, a

18

far better chance than David or Sappho ever had
— to communicate his image of life to his contemporaries. Imperfect transmission is to be expected:
errors in perceiving, failure in recording, these
reports of the senses. A short-circuited poet is
as familiar a phenomenon as a short-circuited
preacher. But liability to error does not inhibit
the glorious possibility of the individual's getting
the attention of his generation, and perhaps of
all generations. I once listened to Mommsen the
historian, Ernst Curtius the archæologist, and
the librarian of the University of Berlin, upon the
credibility of human testimony. The librarian
concluded by asserting, "I would rather trust
an inscription upon a stone than a man." But,
one may humbly ask, who carved that stone?
And did the librarian ever happen to read any
inscriptions on tombstones?

In spite of the lurking likelihood to error, written speech thus strives to make permanent its
record of feeling and thought. "Go, stranger, and
tell the Spartans that we died here." Immense is
the pathos of this human endeavor to eternalize
the transient. The wonder is that so much is
remembered: the Law on the tables of stone, the
fragments of Sappho's passion, the story of a few
imperishable deeds. The written word does, in a
fashion, succeed in its undertaking. Even when

languages and races pass, the written words may
survive, if only for the theme of scholars' quarrels
about Etruscan inscriptions, Runic crosses,
Eliot's Indian Bible, George Meredith's "Shaving
of Shagpat." What rich salvage the archæolo-
gists and philologists find in the human wreck!

Yet, after all this is admitted, there is a radical
impermanence arising from the very nature of
language. It is in a perpetual flux of change. It
reflects the "undulating and diverse" quality of
all human experience. However unambiguous the
written word may seem, it is only a symbol of
some "body-and-mind" reaction. These reactions are never identical in two persons, or even in
the same person during successive phases of his
experience. We agree tacitly that words shall
have a sufficiently definite meaning to serve as the
medium of human intercourse. They do. We
cannot be forever weighing and counting and
criticizing these soiled and worn bits of currency.
We pass them over the counter, rejoicing now and
then in a freshly minted piece or sighing over a
tattered rag of phrase worn out in service. How
rarely does a word give an exact and quiet picture
of the thing as it is! "Circular saw" denotes much
the same object to all those who have visual or
tactile memories. The word "sunset" connotes
as many visual images and complexes of emotion

as there are people in the world. These are perhaps extreme examples; and yet precisely what
do we mean by "Darwinism," "consent of the
governed," "back to Nature," "liberty, frater-
nity, equality," "Unitarianism," "Americanism"? Translations of the Bible, the words and
phrases of the historic creeds, illustrate this same
impossibility of fixing in written words the
"body-and-mind" reactions of successive generations. Saint Paul is thought to have had a clear
head, but we cannot tell just what he meant by
the words "resurrection of the body." It is not
strange that artists in bronze and marble think
their work done when it is finished; but the artist
in words is a gambler, who never knows how long
his coin will pass.

Of one thing we may be sure. When the written
word is colored by that image-making quality
which transforms mere language into literature, it
does record human progress. Though it arises
itself out of the turbulence of the senses, it sets up
a mark above the senses' ebb and flow. Like a
terminal moraine, it indicates the former presence
of great phenomena of the temporal and spiritual
worlds. Single words surviving from Greek philosophy, Roman law, mediæval philosophy, betray
what were once the preoccupations of human
society.

And it is not merely the epoch-making general movements that are thus recorded. The written word perpetuates, externalizes — it may be eternalizes — the exceptional experience of those individuals who have thought deeper and soared in their imaginations higher than the crowd. Their intuitions, once fitly expressed, become henceforth the potential experience of all men. We discover at last what Plato and Shakespeare meant, and their words begin to vibrate in us for the first time. Thus the world slowly overtakes, in thought and passion, the experience of the solitary and pioneering individual. When Jefferson catches his vision of Democracy, or Tolstoy perceives that the world of men is one, their words of annunciation are as truly acts as the voyage of Columbus or the signing of the Emancipation Proclamation. What is written by such men stands. Humanity measures its own past progress by it, and by it forecasts the future.

If the written word thus demonstrates the intellectual and spiritual status of races and periods, it is obvious that it is one key to an understanding of civilization. We cannot really know Mexico, Italy, France, Russia — to say nothing of Greece and Rome — without knowing something of their speech. Now, it is true that mere capacity for learning foreign languages — a capacity in which

Americans are weaker than any civilized people except the British — takes one not very far. You may remember Bismarck's cynical advice to the proud father of a boy who spoke several languages. "What shall I make of my linguistically gifted son?" asked the father. "A head waiter," said Bismarck, who was not without linguistic talent himself. I know from personal experience that in the universities of Bismarck's Germany there was an amazing knowledge of the philology of English words, an amazing acquaintance with the external facts of English history, coupled, as I now look back upon it, with a profound ignorance of the English character. These learned Germans did not know England, though they thought they knew her better than she knew herself.

I am not claiming that it is easy to understand the real springs of national life. I do not think that the Americans of the United States understand one another yet, although they all talk "American." Certainly they know little and care little about the Latin-American nations to the south of us, and the masses of our population are as yet unconvinced that our weal and woe will be identical, in the long run, with the weal and woe of Europe. True "international-mindedness" comes slow and hard. Yet it is the only known correction of nationalistic self-justification, self-glorification. That is why I am pleading for a better knowledge of the written words of Europe, as one way of discovering the mind of Europe. What we perpetually need is a sense of the slowly evolved universal standards of public and private conduct. These things cannot be settled in a corner, and certainly not in any one corner of the United States. The verdict of mankind is rendered by an immense jury of thinking men and women, never yet discharged, settling and resettling, by eternal standards, but in the light of advancing knowledge and growing spiritual life, what Rufus Choate called "the great mixed cases of the world."

You will see that I am asking for something more than a mere knowledge of foreign languages, ancient and modern, more than a mere study of international literary influences in a technical sense, as they are already pursued, for example, by comparative literature. Such knowledge of the written word, valuable as it is, is only a preliminary step to a perception of the mind and heart of Europe and of the Orient. It is sadly clear to-day how far apart in spirit the nations of the earth may be, though their ships crowd one another on the ocean routes and their wireless signals web the globe. Without a mutual understanding of national mentality and motives, it is premature

24

to say much about international fellowship. What
I am urging is that cultivation of the national intelligence, that awareness of the mental and moral
processes of other nations, which is possible only
through a heightened respect for literature. It is
bad politics to continue to send ambassadors to
Paris and Berlin who know no word of French
or German; but worse yet is the national self-
complacency which accepts such indifference to
the significance of language and literature as in-
terpreters of civilization.

In this period of world-wide readjustment, we
Americans might as well face the facts. We have
never had in this country — except, perhaps, in
the New England of the seventeenth century —
any widespread and fundamental respect for literature. We respect schools and we endow colleges, but when men like Emerson, Hawthorne,
and Poe venture one step beyond the limits of
school and college sympathy, they are obliged to
stand for long years alone. The American public
has not yet learned to regard such men as objects
of national pride. Our Hall of Fame is more or less
of a newspaper joke. The incorporation of a National Institute of Arts and Letters with its associated Academy was bitterly attacked and repeatedly defeated in Congress as being somehow
undemocratic. The real influence and standing

of a man of letters in any American community is negligible. Most Americans are less proud, at heart, of the world-wide fame of Edgar Allan Poe than of the world-wide ubiquity of a certain kind of car.

I am quite aware that excellent excuses may be offered for this indifference of our public to creative literary art. There are excuses historical and political and political-historical; excuses economic and moralistic and humanitarian, to explain why our preoccupation with other concerns has crowded out the time and thought, the leisure and meditation necessary to the service of the Beautiful and the True. But the fact remains that "backward" Russia is contributing far more to the world's art and literature than these prosperous United States. Who says of any American writer, painter, musician, what a Russian Jew immigrant said to me the other day of Tolstoy: "Tolstoy? The greatest man we had!"

One remedy, surely, lies, not in fault-finding and speech-making, but in the constructive, organized activity of State instruction, beginning at the bottom. The old red schoolhouse — which is gone — did its poor part to make language and literature a vital matter to the life of the community. The old small college — which is going — did its part also. The endowed universities have done relatively less; and the State universities have never yet placed the full resources of the Commonwealth at the service of these liberalizing studies which are essential to the intellectual life of our people. You perceive the vicious circle: we have no vital community faith in linguistic and literary studies; the State universities provide what the taxpayers demand; hence they do not provide what is not demanded. I know that there are many school hours given to what is called "English." But where is even the mother tongue taught with intellectual passion, with a true sense of the mystery and beauty of words, the power and enchantment of great prose and poetry? We need primary teachers who will teach the children of the poor that words are living things. They are battles. Sometimes they are better than battles. Said Cardinal Newman: "If by means of words the secrets of the heart are brought to light, pain of soul is relieved, experience recorded and wisdom perpetuated — if by great authors the many are drawn up into unity, national character is fixed, a people speaks, the past and the future, the east and the west are brought into communication with each other; if such men are, in a word, the spokesmen and prophets of the human family — it will not answer to make light of literature or to neglect its study."

POETRY AND PROGRESS [1]

I

TWELVE years ago the Harvard Chapter of Phi Beta Kappa listened to an address by James Bryce. It was entitled "What is Progress?" Many members of our society will recall their pleasure in following that cautious and dexterous inquiry — "a sort of skirmishing reconnaissance," as the author himself termed it — into the possibility of human advance. For Mr. Bryce was too good a Scotchman to beg the question. With a cool and skeptical intelligence he directed our attention to the present actual condition of mankind, physical, mental, social, and moral, and then he asked us to estimate, in the light of an historian's wide knowledge of the past, whether the race has really progressed. You may remember that Mr. Bryce was confident that what we call material progress has increased, and that there has been an immense gain in knowledge. But he also thought that it was impossible to say whether the creative powers of the human mind — as exhibited in poetry, philosophy, history, for in-

[1] Address before the Harvard Chapter of Phi Beta Kappa, June 16, 1919.

stance — have either improved or deteriorated,
and that it was equally impossible to say whether
there has been any gain in human happiness. His
concluding words were these: "The bark that
carries Man and his fortunes traverses an ocean
where the winds are variable and the currents unknown. He can do little to direct its course, and
the mists that shroud the horizon hang as thick
and low as they did when the voyage began."

Not precisely a jubilant peroration; at least so
it seemed to many of us as we walked home. It
happens that in Lord Bryce's recent volume of
"Essays and Addresses" there is another discussion of the persistent problem, under the title
"War and Human Progress," an address delivered at the University of Birmingham in 1916.
Here the orator attacks the Prussian doctrine of
Force, the theory that the State is Power and is
a law unto itself. As against the two main lines
of argument supporting the doctrine of Power —
the biological and the historical — Lord Bryce
maintains that the law of progress through strife
is not a universal law of human society, and that
no one has succeeded in tracing any causal relation between war and intellectual and moral
achievement. He claims that the chief cause of
the progress of mankind is the exercise of creative
thought. It is thought that has produced litera-

ture, philosophy, art, and religion, the chief things that make life worth living. Hence he concludes that the future progress of mankind lies in friendly coöperation in the healing and enlightening works of peace and in the growth of a spirit of friendship and mutual confidence which may remove the causes of war.

Now it is clear that the address of 1916, although written in a dark hour, is more confident in tone than the address of 1907. It is not only surer of the fact of progress, but of the road by which humanity must travel in order to make further advance. If the clear-sighted author of the "American Commonwealth" could thus deliberately, in 1916, set the hopes and teachings of poets and philosophers, the claims of reason and sympathy, above the arguments for Power, I do not need to apologize to-day for asking you to think of some of the relations between Poetry and Progress.

For it is plain that this case of Progress is still being tried, as it has long been under trial, in two courts at the same time. The judge in one court is what Charles Lamb whimsically called "the Caledonian intellect"; that is to say, logic, argument, or, as New Englanders liked to say in the Transcendental epoch, "the understanding." Are men advancing? The court of the understanding

— and we should not assume rashly that this is
the lower court — gives the Scottish verdict of
"not proven." The court of the imagination,
which claims at least concurrent jurisdiction in
such matters, and which some believe to be the
court of final appeal, both asserts the fact and
expounds the law of progress.

Here, for example, are two verdicts handed
down from the court of the understanding, or, if
you will allow an eighteenth-century phrase, "the
prose-reason." The first is from Buckle's "History of Civilization in England," chapter 4:

The expression, "moral and intellectual progress,"
is suggestive of a serious fallacy. In the manner in
which it is generally used, it conveys an idea that the
moral and intellectual faculties of men are, in the advance of civilization, naturally more acute and more
trustworthy than they were formerly. But this, though
it may possibly be true, has never been proved. It
may be that, owing to some physical causes still unknown, the average capacity of the brain is, if we compare long periods of time, becoming gradually greater;
and that therefore the mind, which acts through the
brain, is, even independently of education, increasing
in aptitude and in general competence of its views.
Such, however, is still our ignorance of physical laws,
and so completely are we in the dark as to the circumstances which regulate the hereditary transmission of
character, temperament, and other personal peculiarities, that we must consider this alleged progress as a

very doubtful point; and in the present state of our knowledge we cannot safely assume that there has been any permanent improvement in the moral or intellectual faculties of man, nor have we any decisive ground for saying that these faculties are likely to be greater in an infant born in the most civilized part of Europe than in one born in the wildest region of a barbarous country.

The second is from the closing passage of Darwin's "Descent of Man":

The main conclusion arrived at in this work, namely, that man is descended from some lowly organized form, will, I regret to think, be highly distasteful to many. But there can hardly be a doubt that we are descended from barbarians. . . . Man may be excused for feeling some pride at having thus risen, though not through his own exertions, to the very summit of the organic scale; and the fact of his having thus risen, instead of having been aboriginally placed there, may give him hope for a still higher destiny in the distant future. But we are not here concerned with hopes or fears, only with the truth as far as our reason permits us to discover it; and I have given the evidence to the best of my ability.

A more upright witness and judge than Darwin there could not be. Yet you will note his words: "We are not here concerned with hopes or fears." Now, it is precisely of the hopes and fears of humanity that the other court, the high court of the imagination, takes cognizance. It asserts the

32

legitimacy of hopes and fears as an integral part of human experience. Let us choose a single province of the imagination, namely, poetry, and ask for its verdict upon the question as to whether men are, upon the whole, making any headway.

II

WE must admit, of course, that there are great fields of poetry which do not concern themselves in the least with this question of progress. Witness the static quality of much Oriental literature. It asserts, with disillusioned finality, that what hath been, it is that which shall be; that there is no new thing under the sun; that man hath no preëminence above a beast. Or witness the frank objectivity, the pure story-telling quality, of the epics. Trojans, Greeks, Volsungs, Burgundians, Franks, pass before us like the figures in a magic mirror, leaving us no wiser as to their destiny or our own. Nor is it always very different with the drama. Shakespeare, as smilingly as Chaucer, puts how many questions by! Was he Catholic or Protestant? Absolutist or liberal? Did he hold that we men are winning or losing? We may guess, but we do not know.

And yet it is obvious that the drama, from Æschylus to Ibsen, has often grappled with this question of progress. Lyric poets, without stop-

33

ping to debate, have flung their passionate evidence into the scales, forgetting for the moment their own fortunes in their absorption with "the doubtful doom of human kind." "I take all great poetry," wrote the late Professor Courthope, "to be not so much what Plato thought it, the utterance of individual genius, half inspired, half insane, as the enduring voice of the soul and conscience of man living in society."

Certainly if poetry be that, it must have something to say about progress. As a matter of fact, we know that it often serves as a register of progress. It records the beginning and the culmination of certain social efforts, such as Liberalism in Russia, Chartism in England, Anti-Slavery in America. It is a revealer of progress or of the lack of progress, inasmuch as it lays bare the thoughts of many hearts. Lyric poetry, at least, has no reticence. If race-hatred, for instance, be in the poet's soul, his verses betray him. But poetry is also a positive factor in progress. It has served to clarify the mind of individuals and of society. It has established certain standards for judging civilization. That it has often proved a social stimulant of high if dangerous potency is well known: witness the "Marseillaise," the "Carmagnole," the "Internationale." But one of its chief functions, after all, and certainly the most signif-

34

icant for confused epochs like our own, is the emphasis which poetry lays upon certain conceptions, certain theories or ideals of society, which are most clearly revealed in the very instant when they seem most threatened, as the lightning flash illuminates the landscape.

I venture to select, therefore, even in this hour of widespread disillusionment and reaction, a few ideals for society which have been proclaimed by poetry. Let us ask ourselves whether these ideals still persist, and whether the poets think that there is any measurable progress toward their attainment.

III

TAKE first, as the most searching of all tests of individual and social progress, the conception of Righteousness. Every race knows the meaning of that word, as every race knows a right angle. We are all aware that a passionate yearning for rightness is expressed in very primitive types of poetry, such as the Hebrew lyric, and that it is there expressed with a simplicity, intensity, and directness unsurpassed in modern verse. This conception of righteousness endures. It becomes more subtle, possibly more subjective, but contemporary poets like Francis Thompson and Mr. Masefield and Mr. Kipling mean by righteousness

exactly what Dante and Milton meant. They not
only assert its transcendent value, but they feel
instinctively that humanity is progressing toward
it. Quite apart from the utterances of distinc-
tively Christian poets like Browning, Tennyson,
and Wordsworth, there is an overwhelming testimony from pagan and heretic and agnostic poets
whose instincts tell them that humanity is on the
march and that righteousness lies somehow at the
end of the journey. Virgil is as confident of it as
Shelley. Collect, if you have the curiosity, from
all the literatures you know, poems built upon
these three symbols: the road, the sea, the dawn.
Now, road-poems, sea-poems, dawn-poems, chosen
from many races and many epochs, are alike at
least in this: they crystallize human experience in
a symbol of endless advance, of widening space,
of broadening light. The end of the quest, the
harbor of the voyage, the high noon of what now
seems but a chill daybreak, is after all what quite
prosaic persons mean when they use the old-
fashioned word righteousness. It is the imagination appealing from the apparent fact of the moment to the truth as seen *sub specie æternitatis*.

IV

LET us turn to another ideal of human society,
scarcely less noble, the ideal of Justice. What do

we mean by it? It is "the interest of all," said
Aristotle; "the will to render every man his right,"
said Ulpian; "the ligament," said Daniel Webster, "which holds civilized beings and civilized
nations together"; or, in the words of a more
recent definition, "Justice is the equilibrium
between the freedom of the individual and the
safety of society." No word, however we may
define it, is more often upon human lips. Yet
there are singularly few poems about justice itself.
An equilibrium is too abstract a theme for poetry.
Mural painters decorate court-houses with pictures
of Justice holding her even scales, but it is commonly Injustice that inspires poetry. "Injustice
cuts to the bone," said an old English judge; and
whatever does that, makes poetry possible. When
the iron enters into the soul, the verses come. It
is the poetic imagination, therefore, as well as the
perplexed reason, which asks whether the Judge
of all the earth does right, whether the eternal law
is one thing at Athens and another at Rome, or
whether it is immutable. If there are few poems
celebrating Justice in the abstract, there are
countless poems which attempt to assail or to
justify the concrete ways of God to man. They
demand why Injustice so often seems triumphant.
They chant the praises of defeated persons and
lost causes. The suffering Prometheus, chained in

37

his rocky cleft in the Caucasus, has inspired finer
poetry than any sworded Seraphim. And nevertheless the poetic imagination, brooding upon
what seems transparent injustice, often recoils
upon itself; it proclaims that Prometheus, and
not the tyrant Jove, is really triumphant, that to
him belongs the future — "Life, Joy, Empire,
and Victory." Even Thomas Hardy's "The Dy-
nasts," a poem of the Napoleonic Wars which
many persons have re-read during the last five
years, and one of the most bitter arraignments of
the general scheme of things drawn by any poet
in our day, closes with a strain of forgiveness
toward the unconscious Will, and with the thrill
of a new hope

"That the rages
Of the ages
Shall be cancelled, and deliverance offered from the darts that
were,
Consciousness the Will informing, till It fashion all things
fair."

But it is in the portrayal of human justice and
injustice that the poets chiefly betray their attitude toward Progress. Our human experiment
cannot be worked out in a vacuum, nor upon a
desert island. As soon as Robinson Crusoe finds
the footprints of another man upon the sand,
the question of justice and injustice begins, and

it develops into what Rufus Choate called "the great mixed cases of the world." How infinitely complicated they become, these woven strands of instinct and custom, of legality and equity, of right and wrong! How impossible it seems to strike a fair balance, to render to each man according to his rights! To the prose-reason it is impossible. When Richardson built the Hampden County Court-House in Springfield, an inscription was desired for the façade. "Justitia" was suggested, but the fastidious Dr. Buckingham said no: justice is an ideal to which man does not attain: let the word be "Lex." And "Lex" it is, cut into the gray stone, to show that while the courts may strive in vain for absolute Justice, they can at least apply the law.

Now, open Browning's "Ring and the Book." A "mixed case," if there ever was one, is this Roman murder story of the seventeenth century, told twelve times over, in different voices, by the cleverest special pleader of the nineteenth century. But this pleader, being a poet, makes sure of both Lex and Justitia. His clear-headed old Pope orders Count Guido to be beheaded, as the only possible way of saving his soul! If Browning's solution be thought too fanciful, pass to those questions of social justice that came to the front in the eighteenth century in England.

In that rebirth of emotion which characterized the age, the poor, the beggar, the outcast, even the criminal, were seen with new eyes. Beneath the polished surface of Gray's "Elegy" there is a passionate recognition of the inequalities of the human lot. Cowper, the quietist, demands the destruction of the Bastille in 1784, five years before the mob of Paris acted. Mobs and legislative enactments and judicial decisions come limping along in due time after the Pre-Revolutionary sentiment of poets. It was the poets, even earlier than the statesmen, who asserted that Napoleon's power could not endure, since it was founded upon injustice. So it was with the poets and novelists in the full current of Victorian humanitarianism: they made the social diagnosis, however wild some of their prescriptions may have been. Legislation followed the imaginative depiction of social wrongs. First comes the sonnet or the novel, afterward the statute. For Mr. Dooley was quite right in his epigram on the Philippine cases, that, whether or not trade follows the flag, the Supreme Court follows the election returns. The community ultimately writes its will into the statutes. Only there is this vast difference between the persons who think of Justice in the terms of statutes and the persons who think of Justice in the terms of poetry: the poets are surer of their ground.

40

Lamartine said of one of Napoleon's judicial murders: "The murderer has but a moment, the victim has eternity." He might have written it of Edith Cavell. If the poets cannot always declare with Carlyle that there is nothing else but justice in the universe, they at least assert the ultimate triumph of justice. They believe that whether you and I win or lose, the "forts of folly" will one day fall. If beaten in the lower court of the understanding, they make their proud appeal to Cæsar, to the imperial rights of the imagination.

V

WE may test the relation of poetry to progress by examining another conception, namely, the ideal of Liberty. That ideal is both individual and social, but its social aspects are more interesting to the present-day world. Men everywhere are striving for freedom in society. It is true, of course, as Shelley maintains in his sonnet on "Political Greatness," that man must first "rule the empire of himself." But even a community of self-rulers must find, after all, some practical equilibrium between the freedom of individuals and the freedom of all. So argues John Stuart Mill in his famous essay on "Liberty," as John Locke had argued in the essay on "Toleration." This conception of Liberty as an equilibrium be-

41

tween extremes is perfectly phrased by Tennyson
in his "Of old sat Freedom on the heights," a
lyric which sets to music the "middle-of-the-road"
philosophy of Burke. The poetry of the Latin
races is rich in praise of Liberty in the abstract,
and Swinburne, an exception in this respect
among English poets, and Walt Whitman, always
an exception among American poets, have di-
lated upon the theme with almost the eloquence
of Victor Hugo.

Yet you will find English poets, like English
orators, more often discussing their liberties —
that is, their legal rights — than Liberty in the
absolute. Our poets of emancipation are forever
chanting about freedom from something, freedom
toward something. They are motor-minded. For
it is unfreedom, like injustice, which stings men
into the wrath that makes verse. We all wish
liberty from oppression, from unjust laws, from
the tyranny of the mob as well as from the tyranny
of Kaisers. But the poets bring to such questions
an insight, an imagination, a partisanship, beyond the grasp of the prose-reason. When Lowell
entreated Whittier to "cry aloud and spare not
against the cursed Texas plot," he appealed to
a specialized sense of outrage as well as to a
specialized power of expression. Ebenezer Elliott,
the Corn-Law rhymer, may have understood the

economic injustice of the Corn Laws less accurately than Cobden, but millions of men sang his rough rhymes and hastened the repeal. Even the mere questioners of society, the Heines, the Ibsens, the Byrons, the Bernard Shaws, the satirists and the mockers, have thus been soldiers in the army of liberation. They have often served the cause better by their plays and songs than by their experiments with actual legislation. That is a delightful story of Béranger, who resigned in disgust his seat in the National Assembly, where Victor Hugo was a fellow-member. A friend remonstrated, saying, "You ought to be proud to serve in the same regiment with Victor Hugo." "He isn't in the regiment," replied Béranger gloomily; "he's only in the band."

But the band led the regiment in 1848, and in 1861 it was not for nothing that Mrs. Howe wrote the "Battle Hymn of the Republic." The fact is that the regiment does not always keep up with the band: if it did, that old Greek story about the songs of a people being more important than their laws would be justified. It is hard for the laws to keep step with the music of the idealists; and the idealists are apt to be more eloquent in their denunciation of wrong than accurate in their sense of direction toward the right. For what are we to do with our liberties after we have won them? The oppressed should go free, certainly, but whither shall they go? Better wages, better hours, better housing are only steps toward something, and toward what? To Emerson, writing his "Boston Hymn," it all seemed clear. The American Commonwealth was at last purged from slavery: Freedom was to be King; the goal was self-mastery for the individual, self-government for the State. The "Boston Hymn" was a good fife and drum for 1863 even though the regiment has never quite kept step with it — for, alas, we Americans still lynch the sons and grandsons of the men set free by the Emancipation Proclamation, and to-day we are moving painfully forward into a new civilization, realizing that even self-mastery and a self-governed United States of America do not of themselves secure the peace of the world.

Yet it is something, surely, that the poets of our race have left us in no doubt of their feeling toward Liberty. In spite of every temporary defeat and disaster they believe that it is coming. They have an instinctive, if not always a logical, faith in progress. Wordsworth wrote of Germany in 1809, while the most learned nation in Europe was lying prostrate before Napoleon at the very moment when a few Tyrolese peasants were rising against him:

44

> "Her haughty Schools
> Shall blush: and may we not with sorrow say
> A few strong instincts and a few plain rules
> Among the herdsmen of the Alps, have wrought
> More for mankind at this unhappy day
> Than all the pride of intellect and thought."

The poetic imagination, you will observe, simplifies this vexed question of Liberty into

> "A few strong instincts and a few plain rules."

I do not claim that poets, any more than other men, are always faithful to their best instincts. Coleridge, in his "Ode to France," renounced his dream of human liberty. But if Coleridge and Southey recanted, Byron and Shelley did not. "Are you really of the whole people?" Whitman asks of American poets, and I think him quite right in maintaining that partialists, alarmists, and infidels to the cause of Liberty have no place in the United States.

VI

I VENTURE finally, and not without a sense of the complications and inherent difficulties of the topic, to test the attitude of poets toward that desire of humanity which we call by the "dear affronted name of Peace." That this is one of the goals of human effort no one doubts, but as to whether we are making any substantial progress toward it there is a widespread skepticism. The very word "Peace" is under suspicion. It means, like so many words that have been the symbols of fierce controversy, diametrically opposite things to different persons. There are men of dynamic temperament to whom "Peace" implies passivity, sloth, negation of personality, defeat of the will. You recall how the Philistine, in the Easter Sunday scene in "Faust," comfortably drains his glass as he remembers that far away in Turkey there is fighting going on. But he is at peace, and he saunters happily homeward. There are other men to whom "Peace" means, not stagnation and indifference, but the harmonious functioning of social and political machinery, efficiency, order, civilization.

Now, both of these types of temperament are found among poets. The poetry of our own race is full of such themes as peace through escape, cloistered peace, the peace of old age, a peace like that of a summer night. There is even a school of contemporary verse-making in this country which denies that social and moral questions, such as those involved in peace and war, have any place whatever in poetry. This school maintains that poetry should deal with surfaces only, with retinal and aural impressions of the individual, and that all generalizations of human experience

46

are out of place in it. "True poetry," wrote one
of these men recently, "is the entering of delicately
imaginative plateaus, unconnected with human
beliefs or fundamental human feelings." At the
opposite extreme we find that body of nationalistic
and imperialistic verse with which we have grown
familiar since the Boer War — "jingo" poetry,
"White man's burden" poetry, hymns of hate and
of racial pride, vainglory and hypocrisy. If we
look too closely at either end of the scale, whether
at dehumanized æstheticism, detached from the
greater interests of mankind, or at mere versi-
fied political passion, we may well doubt whether
poetry can clarify our judgment upon the transcendent question of progress toward peace.

But the chief colors of the spectrum are more
important than the fringes. There is a vast body
of enduring literature, Hebrew, mediæval, and
modern, in which the poetic imagination has
grappled with the conception of peace on earth.
Century after century the great poets as well as
the freak poets have had their say. I have not
the skill to summarize all of their conclusions, but
I will risk two generalizations concerning them.

The first is this. Peace, according to the poets,
is a resultant of other forces. It presupposes the
partial success, at least, of those other ideals of
humanity which we term Righteousness, Truth,

Justice, Liberty, and Fellowship. For Peace, like beauty, is a harmony of effects. It is a commonplace of poetry, as of law and politics, that there can be no permanent adjustment of differences that is not based upon right. Injustice inevitably provokes revolt. Peace must be founded upon truth to fact: otherwise it is but a sham peace, an armed peace. Surely there can be no peace without liberty. Neither can there be any peace without fellowship. Among friends the question of peace does not arise. They do not know what the word "ultimatum" means.

Is it strange, then, that when you ask the poets whether we are really making progress toward peace, they should sometimes mumble, like some old oracle, in unexpected words, in syllables that sound not like "Peace" at all, but, rather, like some harsher word such as "Righteousness," or "Justice," or "Liberty"?

> "Prince Vortigern — so run the ancient tales —
> A stronghold sought to build in wildest Wales;
> But some fell Power frustrated each essay,
> And nightly wrecked the labours of the day;
> Till Merlin came, and bade the builders all,
> Beneath the escarp'd and many-bastioned wall,
> Dig deep; and lo, two dragons, o'er whose lair
> Nothing secure might rise, lay sleeping there.

> "Search the foundations, you that build a State;
> For if the dragon forms of Wrath and Hate

48

Lie coiled below, and darkly bide their hour,
Fear walks the rampart, Fear ascends the tower.
And let it not content you that they sleep:
Drive them with strong enchantments to the deep.
First of such charms is Perfect Justice; then
Comes the heart's word that conquers beasts and men.
No other craft shall serve — no spells but these
Drive the old dragons to the whelming seas."

That poem of William Watson used a Welsh legend to explain contemporary world politics. But to-day we do not need any legends. The newspapers reported, not long ago, the accidental burning of a Japanese temple, famed for its priceless decorations and its roof of gold. A beggar had crawled under it and tried to warm himself by lighting a tiny fire with waste paper. Much of our modern civilization is still like that: a roof of gold and freezing reckless beggars lurking in the underpinning. It is not the poets, it is the sentimental politicians, who cry peace when there is no peace, who argue for our international isolation when such a thing is no longer possible. Preventive medicine studies and removes the causes of disease. Fire prevention means the elimination of inflammable construction, and not merely a gallant fire department which thinks only of fighting fires after they are started. Apply those analogies to world politics. The war poetry of the last five years has wrought one inestimable service: it has

49

told the pitiless truth, not only about the battle-field, but about the wrath and hate and greed that are coiled around the foundations of Europe. It says little of the pomp and circumstance of glorious war; it goes straight to the human facts underlying war; it shows that world peace is conditioned upon the concrete and fundamental issues of Justice, Liberty, and Fellowship. Without these there can be no progress.

And yet my second generalization is this: that the finest voices of contemporary poetry still bid us to lift up our hearts. Poetry has witnessed inconceivable horrors, and it sees the brutal facts of the present situation. We may be sure that poets are even more keenly sensitive than we are to the reactions that follow great national effort, to the world-wide disillusion which so closely resembles the post-Revolutionary pessimism of a century ago. It was after the triumph of Waterloo that Byron wrote bitterly:

"Europe has slaves, allies, kings, armies still."

The poets know even better than we that every perpetuation of hatred is a postponement of peace, and that the hatred we have to fear in the immediate future is not so much the hot, manly hatred of foes who have faced one another on the battle-field, as the cold hatred of non-combatants, the calculated hatred of competitors for world markets. The poetic imagination sees all this, but it also sees something else, and that other thing is the essential thing: namely, the ultimate supremacy of moral forces. When you and I, brethren of Phi Beta Kappa, are depressed over the prevalent violence of the educated classes, over their lack of serenity and poise, their easily wounded vanity, their distrust of idealism, their disloyalty to moral leadership, we may find comfort in the words of Harvard's most distinguished graduate: "In all the encounters that have yet chanced, I have not been weaponed for that particular occasion, and have been historically beaten, and yet I know all the time that I have never been beaten; have never yet fought, shall certainly fight when my hour comes, and shall beat." Emerson wrote that in a prose essay, but he never wrote more like a poet, for he wrote with the long view. Victor Hugo, uttering strange prophecies before the Peace Convention in Brussels in 1848, and Whittier, celebrating that convention in a poem about

"The great hope resting on the truth of God,"

were, if you like, historically beaten. But the chief question is, after seventy years, were Hugo and Whittier right or wrong? If we think them right, were they ever really beaten? And seventy years hence, as Harvard men meet here, what will they say of our present American effort to insure the peace of the world through a League of Nations? Will they call it wrong, or right?

Poetry, we may be sure, will take the long view of it.

"Not yet, dejected though thy cause, despair,
  Nor doubt of Dawn for all her laggard wing.
  In shrewdest March the earth was mellowing,
  And had conceived the Summer unaware.
  With delicate ministration, like the air,
  The sovereign forces that conspire to bring
  Light out of darkness, out of Winter, Spring,
  Perform unseen their tasks benign and fair.
  The sower soweth over vale and hill,
  And long the folded life waits to be born;
  Yet hath it never slept, nor once been still:
  And clouds and suns have served it night and morn;
  The winds are of its secret council sworn;
  And Time and nurturing Silence work its will."

---

[1] "To One Espousing Unpopular Truth," by William Watson.

DANA'S MAGICAL CHANCE

THE popular impression of Richard Henry Dana is that he was a man of one book. Such impressions are not always infallible, and yet the offhand, instinctive judgment upon which they rest is usually right enough for all practical purposes. In Dana's case the popular verdict is not likely to be reversed. It is one of the ironies of literature that this son of a poet, inheriting so much that was finest in the old New England culture, a pupil of Emerson, trained at Harvard, toiling gallantly in a great profession, a public-spirited citizen of a Commonwealth which he served nobly and without much tangible reward, should be chiefly remembered by his record of an enforced holiday in his boyhood — by what he himself called a "parenthesis" in his life.

But the irony, as happens so often with irony, serves to reveal a fundamental law. It explains this author's nature. In that "parenthesis," as in the parenthesis or postscript of many of our private letters, Dana unconsciously expressed himself. His two years as a common sailor offered him the magical human chance, and he took it. There was something in him for which the deco-

53

rous and conventional life of Boston, in the thirty years preceding the Civil War, allowed no place in its scheme. "Two Years Before the Mast" belongs to the literature of escape. In as true a sense as Thoreau's "Walden" or Parkman's "Oregon Trail" it is a record of an excursion into the uncivilized, the actual; or, as Robert Louis Stevenson puts it, "not the shoddy sham world of cities, clubs, and colleges, but the world where men still lead a man's life." Here Dana could truly express himself, although self-expression was one of the last things that he had in mind. He intended a descriptive narrative of objective fact, "to present the life of a common sailor at sea as it really is," and the task was perfectly suited to his simple, earnest nature, to his lucid mind and style, to his self-forgetful interest in men and things that lay beyond the horizon of conventionality.

He was fortunate, then, in the relation of his theme to himself. It was adapted to his powers of observation and description, congenial to his natural tastes and sympathies. The real romance of adventure revealed itself gradually to a temperament hitherto chiefly responsive to the note of literary romanticism. Books had prepared the way. Young Dana knew his Spenser and Byron, Wordsworth and Scott. It is characteristic of his

54

generation that he finds Robinson Crusoe's island, on his outward voyage, "the most romantic spot on earth" his eyes had ever seen; that "San Juan is the only romantic spot in California," and that he experienced here a "glow of pleasure at finding that what of poetry and romance I ever had in me had not been entirely deadened by the laborious and frittering life I had led"; that the solitary grave of the English captain at San Pedro "was the only thing in California from which I could ever extract anything like poetry." His heart beats fast when he discovers at San Pedro a volume of Scott's "Pirate," and when he finds at San Diego, at the bottom of a sea-chest, Godwin's "Mandeville, a Romance," he drinks delight as from a "spring in a desert land." Very real to him was this romantic sentimentalism, and very characteristic of a bookish boy in the year 1835. But was it true that only in such moods lurked the spirit of poetry? Dana's own narrative answers him with a triumphant negative. The unconscious element of his story has outlasted the self-conscious. How about sending down the royal yard in Monterey Harbor, when the "well done" of the mate gave him as much satisfaction as he ever felt at Cambridge on seeing a "*bene*" at the foot of a Latin exercise? How about running the surf at Santa Barbara? Or swinging off a four-

hundred-foot cliff, at San Juan, on a pair of hal-
yards to save a few hides, and being told for
his pains: "What a d——d fool you were to risk
your life for half-a-dozen hides!" How about furl-
ing the ice-covered jib while drenched with the
long combers off Cape Horn? To Richard Dana's
straightforward mind such things were all in the
day's work. They were duties that must be done,
and he did them, as he described them, in all
simplicity. He told the pedagogic Horace Mann
that his book "had life," but he could not then
realize that to a later generation, taught by Kipling and Conrad, this very day's work was the
essence of romance, while the glimpse of Robinson
Crusoe's island and the lonely California grave of
the forgotten Englishman were only its accidents,
its mere fringe of literary association.

Another good fortune lay in the obvious frame-
work and sequence of the story. Like Defoe's
most famous narrative, it had its natural beginning, its natural series of climaxes, and its due
return to the starting-point. No artificial literary
plot could be better curved than that outward
voyage of the brig Pilgrim in August, 1834, the
timeless sojourn in the new land of California,
then the long beat homeward of the ship Alert
around the Horn and up past the Equator and
into Boston Harbor in September, 1836. Fact is

an artist, though not always the master artist, and in Dana's case fact served him as faithfully as the north star. He made his selections, of course, from the diary of experience, but that instinct for the essential point, which afterward made him a good lawyer, is evident in the orderliness with which he presents the cardinal features of a complex situation. He was not tempted, like some greater writers of the sea, such as Pierre Loti and Conrad, into over-subtlety. He is sometimes, like Kipling, over-technical, but it is due to an honest boyish enthusiasm for the right name of every rope.

Dana was fortunate, above all, in his youthfulness. He wrote at twenty-two. The "parenthesis" did not come, as it comes to many men, even if it comes at all, too late in their life-sentence. "Yet we were young" is the best comment upon the hardships of himself and his companions in California. "Yet we were young"; young enough to "like anything in the way of variety," to feel that the prospect of a change "sets life in motion." Nothing is more touching in Dana's later diaries and correspondence than his belief that this gift of youth, under different circumstances, might still be perennially his. He writes at the age of thirty-nine, after a sailing voyage to the Maine coast: "I believe I was made for the

57

sea and that all my life on shore is a mistake. I was intended by nature for a general roamer and traveler by sea and land, with occasional edits of narratives, and my duties as lawyer, scholar, and publicist are all out of the way." Years afterward he writes to his wife from Minnesota: "We ought to have been travelers; had no profession and no home, and roamed over the world together, like two civilized and refined gypsies." "My life has been a failure," he wrote in 1873, "compared with what I might and ought to have done. My great success — my book — was a boy's work, done before I came to the Bar." His sojourn at Castellamare in May, 1881, a few months before his death, seemed to him "a dream of life." Such confessions as these are the outbreak of an essentially romantic temperament, forced by external circumstances to compete with the persons whom he described perfectly in his first book as the people who never walk in but one line from their cradle to their grave. Boston was full of such people then, as it is still.

One cannot say whether Dana would have been happier had his desire for a life of romantic travel been granted. Certainly he was denied that other dream of his, equally romantic, equally like certain moods of Chateaubriand, in which Dana, who sighed and wept all day over Charlotte Yonge's

"Heir of Redclyffe," desired to give himself "to contemplation, to religious exercises, to nature, to art, to the best of reading and study." This, too, was not to be. He was disappointed, said his law partner, Mr. Parker, in every high ambition of his life. But to dwell upon this phase of his human hunger for the food that is just out of reach is to forget the great good luck of his boyhood, that golden parenthesis of nineteen to twenty-one, to which he chiefly owes to-day the place he holds in human memory.

I am not forgetful, of course, and no one who has read Dana's published work can be unmindful, of the literary excellence of his miscellaneous writings. He was always the master of a clear, direct, and vigorous style, warmed by broad sympathies and sometimes heightened by passionate feeling. His arguments for the reading of the Bible in public schools, on the Judiciary, and on the Rendition of Anthony Burns are notable even in a generation of notable addresses. The fine irony of his attack upon Webster in the imaginary "Great Gravitation Meeting," the acute perception and masculine force of his "Grasp of War" speech, his exhaustive "Note on the Monroe Doctrine," his ingenious though unsuccessful argument before the Halifax Fishery Commission, in which he describes the men of Gloucester as

vividly as Burke, three quarters of a century
before, had described the deep-sea fishermen of
the Atlantic — these are characteristic examples
of his learning and eloquence. His delightful
narrative of a brief journey "To Cuba and Back"
exhibits his dispassionate grasp of complicated
political and social conditions, the free play of an
acute and orderly intelligence. To those who infer
that Dana's harassed and overburdened mature
life was without gleams of imagination, let me
quote one sentence from his eulogy of Rufus
Choate before the Suffolk Bar, that bar that had
listened, not many years before, to Choate's own
eulogy of Webster:

Sir, I speak for myself — I have no right to speak
for others — but I can truly say, without any exagger-
ation, taking for the moment a simile from that element which he loved as much as I love it, though it
rose against his life at last — that in his presence I felt
like the master of a small coasting vessel, that hugs the
shore, that has run up under the lee to speak to a great
homeward-bound Indiaman, freighted with silks and
precious stones, spices and costly fabrics, with sky-
sails and studding-sails spread to the breeze, with the
nation's flag at her mast-head, navigated by the
mysterious science of the fixed stars, and not unpre-
pared with weapons of defense, her decks peopled with
men in strange costumes, speaking of strange climes
and distant lands. . . .

Such writing lingers in the memory, though it be only the memory of a few. But for one American who has read Dana's "Speeches in Stirring Times" there are thousands throughout the English-speaking world who have shared with the boyish Dana his pleasure in the "perfect silence of the sea" and "the early breaking of day on the wide ocean," his awe at "the cold and angry skies" and "long heavy ugly seas" off the Cape, who have seen with him the "malignant" brightness of the lightning in the tropical storm, the yellow California sunshine and the gray California fog, and the slow, stately motion of the groaning Antarctic icebergs with the whirling snow about their summits. Once, on the homeward voyage, there came to him an experience thus described:

One night, while we were in these tropics, I went out to the end of the flying-jib boom, upon some duty, and, having finished it, turned round, and lay over the boom for a long time, admiring the beauty of the sight before me. Being so far out from the deck, I could look at the ship, as at a separate vessel; — and there rose up from the water, supported only by the small black hull, a pyramid of canvas, spreading out far beyond the hull, and towering up almost, as it seemed in the indistinct night air, to the clouds. The sea was as still as an inland lake; the light trade wind was gently and steadily breathing from astern; the dark blue sky was studded with the tropical stars; there was no sound but the rippling of the water under the stem; and the sails were spread out, wide and high; the two lower studding-sails stretching, on each side, far beyond the deck; the top-mast studding-sails, like wings to the top-sails; the top-gallant studding-sails spreading fearlessly out above them; still higher, the two royal studding-sails, looking like two kites flying from the same string; and highest of all, the little sky-sail, the apex of the pyramid, seeming actually to touch the stars, and to be out of reach of human hand. So quiet, too, was the sea, and so steady the breeze, that if these sails had been sculptured marble, they could not have been more motionless. Not a ripple upon the surface of the canvas; not even a quivering of the extreme edges of the sail — so perfectly were they distended by the breeze. I was so lost in the sight, that I forgot the presence of the man who came out with me, until he said (for he, too, rough old man-of-war's man as he was, had been gazing at the show), half to himself, still looking at the marble sails — "How quietly they do their work!"

There, at least, is the magical moment, and what matters it whether the moment comes early or late in a writer's life? It is all the same, said Marcus Aurelius, whether a man looks on these things three years or a hundred. No, it is not quite the same; surely that man is to be envied who has seen the vision of beauty and has had the felicity of recording it, in the days of his youth.

JOHN BURROUGHS [1]

JOHN BURROUGHS was more fortunate than many
"nature writers," in that he was a natural writer.
Audubon, Jefferies, John Muir, and even Thoreau
had slowly to learn the art of composition. But
Burroughs, descendant of Connecticut Yankees,
caught the knack of it easily. He sprang from
plain farming stock and grew up in a household
where books were disregarded. But at seventeen,
when he had begun to support himself by teaching
school, he made his first journey to New York
and returned laden with second-hand volumes —
among them Johnson's "Rambler" and "Idler"
and Saint Pierre's "Studies in Nature." Soon he
was reading E. P. Whipple's essays, and Higginson's, and before long he discovered Emerson.
This went to his head. I remember his talking
with amusement — it was over some steak and
potatoes cooked on the hearth at Slabsides —
about that unsigned essay on "Expression" which
he had published in the "Atlantic" in November,
1860, at the age of twenty-three. Lowell had liked
the essay well enough to print it, and many
readers of the magazine supposed that Emerson
was the author. Yet, aside from a few surface

[1] Read at the Burroughs Memorial Meeting of the American
Academy of Arts and Letters, November 18, 1921.

63

mannerisms, it had no touch of the real Emerson; there was far more of E. P. Whipple and of the amiable author of "Paul and Virginia."

Nearly five years passed before his next contribution to the "Atlantic." This appeared as the leading article for May, 1865, and was entitled "With the Birds." It does not seem written by the same youth who composed the essay on "Expression." The prettily balanced sentences have disappeared, together with the sentimental abstractions. We are now on the actual entrancing earth, watching the thrushes and the hen-hawk. Much had happened to John Burroughs in that interval of five years. He had moved from the headwaters of the Delaware to the banks of the Potomac, and become a Government clerk. He had been reading Wordsworth and Carlyle, Tennyson and Ruskin; and above all he had become a friend of Walt Whitman, who was then engaged in hospital service in Washington. Whitman flung many a door of the spirit wide open for John Burroughs, and the younger man rewarded the friendship by making Whitman the theme of his first book.

The out-of-doors essays now collected in "Wake-Robin" were mostly written in the Treasury Building at Washington, in front of the iron vault which Burroughs was guarding. He had a day off on March 4, 1865, but chose to wander in what was then the wilderness of Rock Creek rather than to join the crowd that listened to Lincoln's Second Inaugural Address. He recorded his strolls about Washington and his boyish memories of the Catskills in a clear, graceful style, in which modesty, gentleness, accuracy of observation, and freshness of feeling are the noticeable features. In succeeding volumes of essays — "Winter Sunshine," "Locusts and Wild Honey," and "Birds and Poets" — this pleasant, mellow style is maintained. It rises into eloquence in the essays on Emerson and Whitman. Yet it seems to me that in the "Pepacton" volume, dating from 1881, Burroughs gives the most authentic evidence, not merely of having mastered the craft of essay-writing, but of having found something of his own to say.

Here are two illustrations, from this volume, of modes of writing which Burroughs was to employ for the next forty years. The first is a naturalistic description of the woodchuck:

In form and movement the woodchuck is not captivating. His body is heavy and flabby. Indeed, such a flaccid, fluid, pouchy carcass I have never before seen. It has absolutely no muscular tension or rigidity, but is as baggy and shaky as a skin filled with water. Let the rifleman shoot one while it lies basking on a

sideling rock, and its body slumps off, and rolls and
spills down the hill, as if it were a mass of bowels only.

The second discusses Nature and the Poets:

It is the soul the poet interprets, not nature. There
is nothing in nature but what the beholder supplies. . . .
Is the music in the instrument, or in the soul of the
performer? Nature is a dead clod until you have
breathed upon it with your genius. You commune with
your own soul, not with woods or waters; they furnish
the conditions, and are what you make them. Did
Shelley interpret the song of the skylark, or Keats that
of the nightingale? They interpreted their own wild,
yearning hearts. The trick of the poet is always to
idealize nature — to see it subjectively. You cannot
find what the poets find in the woods until you take
the poet's heart to the woods. . . .

Of these two passages I personally prefer the
one about the woodchuck. It is veracious, clairvoyant. Yet it was the other style, no doubt,
more idealistic, emotional, and refined, which
gave Burroughs his increasing audience. In the
eighteen-eighties American readers were beginning
to be curious about the fowls of the air, and here
was a man who could write as clearly as Gilbert
White, as enthusiastically as Audubon, and without any of the perplexing queerness, the obstinately intrusive individualism of Thoreau.

How delightful, for instance, are the sketches
of England in "Fresh Fields" — especially "A

Hunt for the Nightingale" and "A Sunday in Cheyne Row." Burroughs had been highly stimulated by Carlyle, and he records his moral and intellectual indebtedness as simply as if he were describing a hemlock tree. John Burroughs possessed, in fact, an unusual gift for appreciative criticism. He had his prejudices, of course. His suspicion of academic persons and of orthodox persons was as persistent as Whitman's. No doubt his critical faculties were hampered by his ignorance of other languages than English and by his almost exclusive preoccupation with nineteenth-century writers. And nevertheless, very few of our critics better equipped in scholarship have written more clarifying papers than John Burroughs wrote on Thoreau, on "Science and Literature," on Gilbert White and on Matthew Arnold. All of these are printed in "Indoor Studies."

Take, for instance, the admirable sentences on Thoreau's defective ornithology:

He had not the detective eye of the great naturalist; he did not catch the clues and hints dropped here and there, the quick, flashing movements, the shy but significant gestures by which new facts are disclosed, mainly because he was not looking for them. His eye was not penetrating and interpretive. It was full of speculation; it was sophisticated with literature, sophisticated with Concord, sophisticated with himself. His mood was subjective rather than objective. He was more intent on the natural history of his own thought than on that of the bird. To the last, his ornithology was not quite sure, not quite trustworthy.

In the volume entitled "Literary Values," published in his sixty-fifth year, how lucid and sane is John Burroughs's protest against the sentimental extravagance that characterized English and American writing at the opening of the twentieth century!

Every age will have its own hobbies and hobbyists, its own clowns, its own follies and fashions and infatuations. What every age will not have in the same measure is sanity, proportion, health, penetration, simplicity. The strained and overwrought, the fantastic and far-fetched, are sure to drop out. Every pronounced style, like Carlyle's, is sure to suffer. . . . Things do not endure in this world without a certain singleness and continence. Trees do not grow and stand upright without a certain balance and proportion. A man does not live out half his days without a certain simplicity of life. Excesses, irregularities, violences, kill him. It is the same with books — they, too, are under the same law; they hold the gift of life on the same terms. Only an honest book can live; only absolute sincerity can stand the test of time.

It was a defense of his own method.

Once, when I begged him to write a certain essay, Burroughs replied: "I'd do it, if I could only get 'het up' enough to flow." In the paper entitled "Real and Sham Natural History," printed in the "Atlantic" for March, 1903, his wrath against the nature fakirs boiled up and flowed over. "I was mad when I wrote it," he confessed to me later, "but it is a mistake to show one's anger on such occasions. A smile is more effective than a scowl at such times." He never reprinted this article, thinking it too controversial, but his friend Roosevelt chuckled over it, and in the opinion of most naturalists and scientific men it rendered a highly useful astringent service in that particular decade. He returned to the subject more calmly in the "Ways of Nature" volume in 1905, but his fundamental skepticism of the new school of "unnatural natural history" was betrayed in this apothegm: "Humanize your facts to the extent of making them interesting, if you have the art to do it, but leave the dog a dog and the straddle-bug a straddle-bug."

I recall an instance of John Burroughs's meticulous effort to tell the exact truth, in which he was aided by the distinguished apostle of veracity who then occupied the White House. "Uncle John's" entertaining article on "Camping with President Roosevelt" told how Roosevelt, in his ranching days, had knocked down a half-drunken ruffian.

"I fetched him as heavy a blow under the ear as I could strike," Burroughs reported the President as saying. But when the manuscript came back from the White House, where it had been submitted for verification, the words "under the ear" were blue-penciled out of the copy, and "on the chin-point" was written in, in the President's firmest handwriting. Two sentences later, the President struck out the sentence, "We soon bound him and turned him over to the constable," and substituted the far more exact and vivid phrase, "We hog-tied him and put him in an outhouse." I still cherish that page of manuscript, as an example of how history was written by the collaborative effort of two of our fellow Academicians.

For it should be remembered that Burroughs's achievement as a man of letters had been recognized by his fellow craftsmen in 1905, when he was one of the first men elected to the Academy of Arts and Letters. He had also the distinction of securing in 1916 the Gold Medal of the Institute for his work in the field of essays and belles-lettres. No less than half a dozen volumes in the uniform edition of his writings were composed after he was seventy. His style changed very little. He never overplayed his rhetorical hand. He never needed an "amplifier" to win and hold his audience. He remained the friendly familiar essayist

of the eighteen-sixties, with the same keen eye
and delicate ear, and with a tireless, ever-increas-
ing curiosity about the physical universe and the
ultimate causes of things. If he watched birds
somewhat less as he grew older, he thought more
constantly about geology and astronomy, biology
and physics, and the origin and destiny of man.
He read William James and Bergson and Oliver
Lodge and Osborn and Loeb and Henderson. He
wrote with simplicity and dignity about the vast,
the insoluble problems raised by contemporary
science and philosophy. He even ventured upon
the field of theology, although never without some
curious traces of that "village-skeptic" epoch in
our American development, when men of such
individual power as the youthful Lincoln pored
over Volney's "Ruins" and Tom Paine's "Age
of Reason." I speak with affection of the "village-
skeptic" type, since it was one of them, a shoe-
maker who had trained his dog to bark angrily
when the Methodist churchbell rang, who introduced me to the books of Thomas Carlyle. Yet I
think that John Burroughs, like his friend Walt
Whitman, never quite outgrew his boyish suspicion of anything in a black coat.

But if we do not know precisely whence we
came or whither we are going—and Burroughs was
certainly not equipped with any new light upon

that question — he was shrewd enough to interest himself also, in his closing years, in those other and equally insoluble problems: How does the chipmunk dig his hole? And what does he do with the dirt? Bergsons come and go, with their fascinating theories of creative evolution, but here scurries our striped friend the chipmunk all the time, digging and hiding, and our blind eyes cannot catch him at some of the simplest of his devices. Who are we, to get excited over theories of Pantheism? Montaigne, the progenitor of the tribe of essayists, and Emerson, pupil of Montaigne and teacher of Burroughs, would have smiled approvingly at the gravity, the charm, and the wisdom with which the aged Uncle John Burroughs came back to his chipmunks.

He had had a long day of it, mostly in the sunshine. He had his desire: to visit with Nature in homely intimacy; to report his enjoyment in a score of sincere books; to open the eyes of two generations of readers; never to be deflected from his aim; never to play for popularity. All this good fortune he had won, together with the affection of his fellow writers, and the regard of the great public. Few of our men of letters have had a career so consistent. The honey-bees which Burroughs learned to mark in his boyhood had a questing and a homing instinct no surer than his own.

THE COLONEL'S QUALITY

COMPARATIVELY few persons can remember Colonel Thomas Wentworth Higginson when he was not already old in years. He published verse in 1842. When he tried to rescue Sims from the court-house, he was twenty-seven; and that was in 1851. He received his commission as Colonel in 1862, and he was then in middle life. Part of the purely personal interest which he aroused and so amply rewarded was a sort of antiquarian curiosity which he had too much humor not to recognize. Here was one who had touched the hands of the elder gods of our American literature, who had known Emerson, Longfellow, and Whittier while they were still young men; one who had actually attended that half-mythical Boston lecture by Edgar Allan Poe. In the delicate cadences of the closing paragraph of his "Oldport Wharves," Mr. Higginson describes an existence not unlike his own later years:

The superannuated fisherman graduates into an oracle; the longer he lives, the greater the dignity of his experience; he remembers the great storm, the great tide, the great catch, the great shipwreck; and on all emergencies his counsel has weight. He still busies himself about the boats, too, and still sails on sunny

73

days to show the youngsters the best fishing ground. When too infirm for even this, he can at least sun himself beside the landing, and, dreaming over inexhaustible memories, watch the bark of his own life go down.

Compared with the men who were treasured in Colonel Higginson's inexhaustible memories, he himself belonged to the "second growth" of our literature, but he had sprung tall and straight and graciously from the as yet unexhausted New England soil. In the attics of old houses in Salem there may still be seen the wide boards of clear, straight-grained pine, toned to a mellow violin coloring by the stray shafts of sunlight. The prose of Mr. Higginson had that same flawless texture, the same heritage and tinge of sunshine. His style matured very early. It was already perfected when he wrote the gay, supple, singing "Charge with Prince Rupert." It is as difficult to date one of his essays by the test of its style as it is to date one of Aldrich's songs or Longfellow's sonnets. "The long centuries," Higginson once wrote, "set aside all considerations of quantity, of popularity, of immediate influence, and sternly test by quality alone — judge each author by his most golden sentence, and let all else go." This test of quality is precisely the one by which the lover of Colonel Higginson's work would wish it to be tried. He wrote hundreds of golden sentences.

74

He did not have the fortune, like his friend
Mrs. Howe, to win fame by one ecstatic lyric, or,
like Wasson and Ellery Channing, to be remembered by one famous line. Though an accomplished orator, he never, like Phillips in Faneuil
Hall, made a name by a single speech. Yet there
is quality throughout Higginson's prose and his
slender pages of verse, and there is rich variety.

It would be hard to find in American literature
any nature essays which surpass his "Water
Lilies," "Footpaths," and "A Summer Afternoon"; an ethical essay more tonic than "Saints
and Their Bodies." We have had no biographical
essay more wholly admirable than the "Theodore
Parker," and certainly none more delightful than
the "John Holmes"; while a more clever controversial essay than Higginson's "Ought Women to
Learn the Alphabet?" has not been written since
the alphabet came into general use. Higginson
served his State and his College as historiographer
and his "Young Folks' History" was something
far more than a perfunctory task. He coasted by
the shores of Romance in "Malbone" and "The
Monarch of Dreams"; the last a powerful sketch
closing with the train of recruits roaring off for the
great war, to reveal, like the bugle-notes and ban-
ners in Arnold's poem, the futility of the "shy
recluses" who cannot follow. Since the Preface

to the "Mosses from an Old Manse" was written
we have had no descriptive sketches more worthy
of comparison with Hawthorne's than Higginson's
delicious "Oldport Days." I do not know whether
anybody is reading them just now, or, for that
matter, whether anybody is reading the Preface
to the "Mosses"; but there the pages are, and
neither Hawthorne nor his pupil will find many
gentler or sunnier pages in the Elysian Fields.

Mr. Higginson tested repeatedly his gifts as a
biographer. Nothing that he wrote in this field
fails in grace, in sound judgment, or in fullness of
knowledge. The "Whittier" and the "Longfellow," however, were both written in his advanced
age, and there was not much that was new to say.
His "Life of Margaret Fuller" remains the most
notable of his studies of other authors: a baffling,
difficult book to write, and a wise and penetrating book to read.

In "Army Life in a Black Regiment" we touch
autobiography. The narrative is as vivid a transcript of experience as Dana's "Before the Mast"
and Parkman's "Oregon Trail," and in neither of
those better-known books is there a better chapter
than Higginson's "Night in the Water." The
whole book demanded tact and humor, a sense of
human and historical values, and a professional
pride in which the Colonel of the First South

Carolina Volunteers was never wanting. I remember that upon one of the last occasions when he attended a meeting of the Massachusetts Historical Society a paper was read demonstrating the ignorance and illiteracy of the negroes of the South Atlantic States, who, we were assured, could scarcely speak or even understand English. The veteran Colonel of the First South Carolina rose very unsteadily to his feet, and made this perfect reply: "My men could understand *me*, when I gave the word, '*Forward!*'"

To praise Higginson's "Cheerful Yesterdays" is to praise him, so perfectly was it a part of him; not the mere inevitable and unconscious betrayal of the personality of an author; but the unconditional surrender of it to the minds and hearts of his friends! For Mr. Higginson was one of those fortunate writers who could transfer to his pages the whole of his personal character. You can no more subtract from his books his idealism, his consistent courage, his erect Americanism, than you can subtract Sir Philip Sidney's knightly qualities from his essay on the nature of poetry. Mr. Higginson loved children and all innocent things. He was chivalrous, not merely toward women — which is easy — but toward "woman" — which is somewhat more difficult. His wit had always a touch of tartness for the American *parvenu;* for he had lived long in Newport and was a good field naturalist. His satire also amused itself with the Englishmen who could not understand what our Civil War was fought for. But in general, Mr. Higginson's list of antipathies was not much longer than such a list should be. Surrounded all his life by reformers, he had, like Emerson, a shrewd detached sense of the eccentricities of reformers. He wrote an amusing essay about it. Many of us have seen him bare his noble gray head when he entered a polling booth, but he never took off his hat to any mere vulgar political or literary majority. To the very end, he remained what Europeans call an "eighteen-forty-eight" man; he carried that old idealism serenely through the demoralized American epoch of the eighteen-eighties and nineties into the new idealistic current of to-day. It is no wonder that he was idolized by the young.

Yet his good fortune lay not merely in this identification of his character with his work as a man of letters. He was also fortunate in settling upon a form of literature precisely adapted to the instincts of his mind. He was a born essayist and autobiographer. Too versatile a workman — and too dependent upon his pen for bread — to confine himself to his true *genre*, he still kept returning to it, like the homing bee. The flexibility of

the essay form, its venturesomeness, its perpetual
sally and retreat, tempted his happy audacity.
But beneath the wit and grace and fire of his
phrases, there is the fine conservatism of the
scholar, the inimitable touch of the writer whose
taste has been trained by the classics. His essays
on "An Old Latin Text-Book" and "Sunshine
and Petrarch" reveal the natural bookman. That
style of his — light and flexible as a rod of split
bamboo — is the style of many of the immortal
classics and humanists; and it holds, when the
bigger and coarser styles warp and weaken. We
speak sometimes of the "charm" of "Cheerful
Yesterdays" as if charm were something external
and evanescent, but the history of literature is
forever reminding us that the charming books
have secret qualities which make them often survive the greater books, just as Cleopatra outshines
the pyramids.

One likes to think, then, of Colonel Higginson,
first as a local figure, to be celebrated by local
pieties. He was loyal to Cambridge. He wrote
poetry about the "Sea Gulls at Fresh Pond"; he
was a true "Child of the College." He drank tea,
in due ceremonial, with all of us. In his old age he
enjoyed the flowers on his birthdays, the tributes
from his clubs, the pleasant notices in the "Evening Transcript." But the negroes who bore his

coffin, and the aliens in religion and race who have as good an eye as anybody for a Puritan man, knew that Colonel Higginson was far more than a local personage. The tea-drinking coteries cannot keep him. Literature will not surrender him to the kindly memory of his neighbors, to the reformers, or even to the veterans of the great war. Higginson lived and died a man of letters. For the claims of literature he gave up the pulpit; to literature he returned when he resigned from the army; and literature will have the final word to say about him. The stone-built court-house is torn down; his description of the attack upon it endures.

No contemporary of any writer can solve what Higginson once called "the equation of fame." That equation contains too many unknown quantities. Lamb's "Essay on Roast Pig," which has simply a good deal of Charles Lamb in it, is now as sure of immortality, as far as we can see, as Gibbon's "Decline and Fall of the Roman Empire." At least we can say: Here are a dozen volumes into which Thomas Wentworth Higginson has put a great deal of himself: clear-grained, seasoned, sun-bathed stuff. They will outlast our day, and many days.

EMERSON'S MOST FAMOUS SPEECH

I

LET us go upon a literary pilgrimage. The shrine which we are to visit is sacred in the memory of scholars, although Mr. Howells, with dispassionate candor, once described it as the ugliest spot in the universe of God. It is Harvard Square. Eighty-six years ago — or, to be precise, on August 31, 1837, Phi Beta Kappa day — it was not without a certain tranquil, rural beauty. Great elms shadowed the little green, in whose center stood a town pump quite after the taste of Hawthorne — although very few Phi Beta Kappa men chose to utilize it on anniversary days, to the scandal of the water-drinking minority. Northwestward from the Square runs the broad road to Lexington and Concord, and on the left, opposite the low-fenced Harvard Yard, is the meeting-house of the First Parish. This edifice, completed in 1834, was the successor of that log meeting-house where just two hundred years before, in the summer of 1637, Anne Hutchinson had been brought to trial by the New England Theocracy, and condemned to exile. If any ghosts of the past are hovering in the First Parish Church on this August morning of 1837, surely among them is the amused ghost of that clever woman, waiting to see what will happen to a new champion of rebellion.

Here, then, is our shrine, a plain wooden meeting-house in a country village, built big enough for the modest needs of Harvard University on its anniversary occasions. Let us march toward it in the procession of our Phi Beta Kappa brethren, two hundred and fifteen strong, starting at twelve o'clock precisely from University Hall, in the middle of the Harvard Yard. Preceded by a band of music and the dark-gowned undergraduate members, the black-coated double file of graduate members emerge from the Yard, cross the road — the dust has been laid by the unwonted rain of the previous day — and halt in front of the meeting-house. The undergraduates open to the right and left, and the President of Phi Beta Kappa, the secretary, chaplain, orator, and poet enter in that order, followed by the members, two and two, according to seniority. Brother John Pierce, D.D., of Brookline (Harvard, 1793), indefatigable attendant and note-taker of Harvard anniversaries, will describe the occasion — an epoch-making occasion, although he did not suspect it.

For, let me warn you, before quoting his record of Phi Beta Kappa's most famous day, that the excellent Brother Pierce has a blind spot in those shrewd old eyes of his, and that his mind is beautifully fortified against doctrines which he disapproves. In that unhappy division of the Congregational churches which had absorbed so much of the attention of New England for thirty years, Dr. Pierce stands for Orthodoxy, and year by year, at Harvard Commencements, he has found himself in an ever-diminishing minority. He computes the reckoning annually, and only yesterday, on August 30, 1837, he has discovered that among Harvard graduates in the active ministry there are one hundred and twelve Liberals to but fifty-one of the Orthodox. Like every true New Englander, no doubt, he felt that the growing unpopularity of his opinions was the best confirmation of their soundness. His passion for oratory never abated, though he lived to attend sixty-four Commencements, but from the beginning to the end of his career, Brother Pierce was suspicious of every intellectual or spiritual novelty.

Aside from this air-tight characteristic of the good man's mind, he is an admirable critic. He sums up Brother Pipon's Phi Beta Kappa Oration of 1803 in one line: it "consisted of miscellaneous and severely critical remarks on Man." I seem to have heard Brother Pipon's oration myself! Dr. Pierce usually characterizes the prayers with which the Phi Beta Kappa ceremonies opened. They are "appropriate," or "pertinent," or "pertinent and judicious," or, at least, "4 minutes" long, or "12½ minutes" long; but I regret to say that, in 1804, when Emerson's father — a well-known Liberal — acted as chaplain, Brother Pierce contented himself by recording: "Dr. Emerson then prayed." In 1836 he is still watching the chaplain with the ear of a heresy-hunter: "The Rev. George Ripley [Harvard, 1823] offered an elaborate prayer of 13 minutes, elegantly composed and expressed. In my mind it was deficient in not giving sufficient prominence to the name which is above every name." Dr. Pierce's instinct was justified by the event: two years later, George Ripley will be found defending Emerson's "Divinity School Address"!

The good Doctor, in short, had, like all of us, the defects of his qualities, as a listener to poetry and oratory. He confesses it with admirable frankness. In 1811 he notes: "John Stickney, Esquire, delivered an oration, of three quarters of an hour, on The Qualifications of a Statesman. Through the course of it I reproached myself with the obtuseness of my faculties, as there was so large a portion of it of which I could not form the trace of a conception. But upon mentioning my

difficulty to intelligent men, I found that I was
not alone. In short, I could compare it to nothing
more striking than a dark night now and then
enlightened by flashes of lightning."

In 1818, according to Brother Pierce, Caleb
Cushing delivers a Phi Beta Kappa poem "on I
cannot tell what." In 1821 the poem by William
C. Bryant, Esq., "was in Spenserian measure and
contained some fine passages. But I was unable
to discern a unity of design or precision of subject.
It was 25 minutes long." Brother Pierce had, at
any rate, an excellent watch! In 1833 he notes:
"Prof. Longfellow, of Bowdoin College, gave a
poem, I know not on what subject, of 28 minutes.
He is a young, handsome man, son of Hon.
Stephen Longfellow, Portland, Harvard University, 1798."

II

BUT while you and I have thus been lingering
over the mental peculiarities of the Reverend
Doctor John Pierce, the black-coated procession
is pushing steadily into the crowded church, and
up the aisles to the seats of honor. As the band
plays its opening voluntary, you may look, if you
like, upon the captains of Israel in their high
places. There is President Josiah Quincy (Harvard, 1790), a vigorous gentleman of sixty-five;

85

the fire of his youthful congressional eloquence
already half forgotten.

Among the Fellows of the Harvard Corpora-
tion, you will note two of the foremost lawyers
of the Commonwealth, Joseph Story and Lemuel
Shaw. Among the Overseers one seeks instinctively
for the well-known faces of John Quincy Adams,
and the great Dr. Channing and the "Godlike"
Daniel Webster. No need to point out the last, in
any assembly of New Englanders; you have but to
follow the eyes of the crowd. But perhaps these
Overseers are absent to-day — since the Phi Beta
Kappa orator is only a stickit-minister from
Concord, author of an anonymous, unintelligible,
and unsold little book on "Nature"!

The Faculty of Harvard College are no doubt
in their places, as in duty bound, unwearied by
the prolonged Commencement exercises of the
previous day. The last name upon the Faculty
list this year is that of the half-crazed, half-
inspired tutor of Greek, Jones Very, of Salem,
poet, who is known to idolize the orator. There
are "the stern old war gods" of the Divinity
School, the Henry Wares, father and son, and
J. G. Palfrey, who a year later are to shake their
heads in awful but belated protest against Waldo
Emerson's astounding utterance to their own
pupils, in their very chapel. There is Andrews

Norton, now retired from his professorship to the watchful leisure of Shady Hill. Just twenty years ago, as Librarian of Harvard College, he had allowed "Emerson 4th" of the Freshman class, "President Kirkland's Freshman" — a sedate, silent youth — to draw the books of Hume and Priestley and other eighteenth-century thinkers; and here is that very Freshman ready now to utter doctrines which Andrews Norton is soon to characterize as "The Latest Form of Infidelity." Let the Wares and the Nortons listen closely this noon; if they do, they will at least be qualified to say in 1838: "I told you so! I knew it, when I heard his Phi Beta Kappa address!"

But amid all the learning and fashion and beauty which throng the meeting-house, do not overlook the eager boys — for their ears catch overtones and undertones which are unperceived by their elders. You will find two or three Cambridge boys whom you know; one a handsome dreamy Senior who had made an eloquent Coleridgian graduating speech the day before, young Richard H. Dana, home for a year now after his "Two Years Before the Mast"; the other is a reckless, irreverent Junior — not yet exiled to Concord by the Faculty — James Russell Lowell. One Concord boy, we may be sure, is here: grave David Henry Thoreau, graduated yesterday, and fairly certain to celebrate his new liberty by going blackberrying to-day, were it not for his desire to hear a fellow townsman speak. You will recognize, perhaps, among the alumni members of Phi Beta Kappa, the high-bred face of a young Boston lawyer, without clients and reputed to be without ambition, who, nevertheless, within four months of this day and by a single impromptu speech will win his place in the front rank of American orators — Brother Wendell Phillips, of the class of 1831. And there is a garrulous Boston Sophomore who ought to be here — Edward Everett Hale; yet if he had been there he would surely have talked about it to the end of his days, and I cannot remember that he ever mentioned it. Probably he was swapping stories outside the church.

And now the music of the brass band blares out into silence at last, and the great audience hushes itself. The Reverend Mr. Rogers of Boston offers a prayer which wins the full approval of Brother Pierce, being "singularly devout, short and appropriate." Then, introduced by the President of the Society, rises the speaker of the day.

Let us look at him as he was then — and with the eyes of that audience — not as we know him now in marble and bronze, gleaming with the serene light of earthly immortality. He is a tall, thin man of thirty-four, with sloping shoulders, a man born, you would say, like his ancestors for seven generations, to wear black. His face is asymmetrical. Seen from one side, it is that of a shrewd New England farmer; from the other, it is a face of a seer, a

> "Prophetic soul of the wide world
> Dreaming on things to come."

The cheeks are fresh-colored, like those of all the Emersons. The thin hair is brown. The eyes are deep blue, with violet lights. He stoops a trifle as he arranges his manuscript upon the pulpit. His manner, though slightly constrained, is suave and courteous. No one in that church, as the Reverend Mr. Emerson pronounces the conventional words "Mr. President and Gentlemen," doubts for a moment his ability to deliver an acceptable discourse. Indeed, he had delivered the Phi Beta Kappa poem, three years before. He belonged, as Dr. Holmes said afterward, to the academic races. This is no amateur, but a professional.

As his clear sweet voice enunciates decorously his opening sentences, the elder Bostonians present are reminded, no doubt, of his father, the gifted minister of the First Church, whose premature death in 1811 had left his boys for a while to the charity of the parish. Chief Justice Shaw, there among the Overseers, had boarded with the widow Emerson on Beacon Street, while she was trying to educate her boys in the Latin School, and perhaps the Justice remembers at this moment the clever poem on Liberty which little Waldo had written in that winter of 1815. Judge Shaw has kept it, and the manuscript is in the Harvard Library to-day.

Possibly the memories of the still older generation go back to the speaker's grandfather, the Reverend William Emerson of Concord, patriot chaplain in the Revolution, and a beautiful pulpit orator, like all that tribe. One listener, I am sure, is thinking of the grandfather, namely, old Dr. Ezra Ripley, of Concord (Harvard, 1776), who had married the chaplain's widow and succeeded him as master of the Old Manse, where the little Emerson boys had spent their vacations with their grandmother. Tough old Ezra Ripley is eighty-six now, but he can still drive himself to Cambridge in his sulky, and it will be some years yet before Waldo Emerson will write his obituary and Hawthorne move into the empty Manse. We know now what Emerson thought of him, but I wish I knew what the old champion of Orthodoxy thinks of Emerson as he sits there in the front pew, revolving many things in his kindly heart.

I fancy that the Harvard professors watch the speaker with a curious and perhaps patronizing interest. He owed them little enough. Kirkland, who had been so kind to him in Wadsworth House, is gone, broken before the time. But there sits Professor Edward Tyrrel Channing ("Ned Channing"), who had corrected Emerson's college themes, and Professor Everett, who had set him an elaborate, and for a while a compelling, pattern for public utterance. And, indeed, the boy had won Bowdoin prizes for essays and a Boylston prize for declamation. But he had otherwise gained no distinction in College, had been the seventh choice of his classmates for the position of Class Poet, and was graduated with a rank of thirtieth in a class of fifty-nine. He was not even, in College, a member of Phi Beta Kappa! His younger brothers, Edward and Charles, won that honor easily. Perhaps there are born candidates for Phi Beta Kappa — as some boys are born to bring flowers to the school-teacher; indeed, the "Harvard Advocate" suggested not long ago that the boy who brings flowers to the teacher becomes naturally a Phi Beta Kappa man. It is the old story: Christopher Wordsworth wins all the prizes at Trinity College, Cambridge, while William Wordsworth reads "Clarissa" during the week preceding the examinations, and barely gets a degree. Both Christopher and William have their reward.

If the professors in Harvard College looked askance at Emerson that day, surely the professors of the Divinity School could have done no less. Ask Professor Henry Ware, Senior, who had "approbated" Emerson to preach, at the end of a broken and disappointing career in the Divinity School. "If they had examined me," said Emerson afterward, "they never would have passed me." Professor Henry Ware the younger had been Emerson's colleague in the pastorate of the Second Church in Boston. There, too, had been failure — as the world counts failure: a decorous performance of duty for a brief period, ending in an irreconcilable difference of opinion between pastor and people regarding the celebration of the communion, and in the pastor's resignation. Illness and private sorrow had been added to professional chagrin: his young wife had died; he had sought change and rest in Europe; he had returned and settled down in Concord to make a scanty living by lecturing and occasional preaching. Sorrow still waylaid him; robbed him of these two brilliant prize-winning brothers, Edward and Charles. But he had pulled himself together, being of the old unbeatable Puritan stuff; he had married again, had bought a house, had published a little book, had backed himself to win against his generation — against the world; and here he is, a sweet-faced, tranquil-voiced man, facing the most distinguished audience that could then be gathered in America, to annunciate his new vision of the eternal Truth. What are his chances of triumphing? I do not believe that his friend Henry Ware, Jr., much as he liked Emerson personally, thought that he had one chance in a thousand. But we talk too much about chances: one chance is enough, if you have the right moment and the man. "All that a man ought to ask for in life," said the French etcher Méryon, "is the chance to put himself into his plates." That supreme felicity was Emerson's, in that August noontide of long ago. He put himself into the oration on "The American Scholar."

I do not say that he won everybody in that packed meeting-house. Certainly he did not convince our hard-headed Brother John Pierce, sitting there on a front seat immovable and unconvincible — watch in hand. Listen to his impression of the address; but listen respectfully, for he is an honest man, and he utters the verdict of the older generation:

Rev. Ralph Waldo Emerson gave an oration, of 1¼ hour, on The American Scholar. It was to me in the misty, dreamy, unintelligible style of Swedenborg,

Coleridge, and Carlyle. He professed to have method; but I could not trace it, except in his own annunciation. It was well spoken, and all seemed to attend, but how many were in my own predicament of making little of it I have no means of ascertaining. Toward the close, and indeed in many parts of his discourse, he spoke severely of our dependence on British literature. Notwithstanding, I much question whether he himself would have written such an apparently incoherent and unintelligible address, had he not been familiar with the writings of the authors above named. He had already, in 1834, delivered a poem before the Society.

And now farewell to Brother Pierce — though he lives to attend eleven more meetings of the Society. The good man had his chance, too!

III

I MUST call three other witnesses to the effect of the oration, familiar to many of you as their testimony may be. Let us hear first a clever young Boston doctor, son of the minister of the First Church in Cambridge and brought up in its gambrel-roofed parsonage. He was the pet and the glory of the class of 1829. He had delighted the Phi Beta Kappa Society with his poem in 1836. He is not yet the "Autocrat," but he knows his own mind and the mind of the younger generation. Oliver Wendell Holmes testifies:

This grand Oration was our intellectual Declaration of Independence. Nothing like it had been heard in the halls of Harvard since Samuel Adams supported the affirmative of the question, "Whether it be lawful to resist the chief magistrate, if the commonwealth cannot otherwise be preserved." It was easy to find fault with an expression here and there. The dignity, not to say the formality of an Academic assembly was startled by the realism that looked for the infinite in "the meal in the firkin; the milk in the pan." They could understand the deep thoughts suggested by "the meanest flower that blows," but these domestic illustrations had a kind of nursery homeliness about them which the grave professors and sedate clergymen were unused to expect on so stately an occasion. But the young men went out from it as if a prophet had been proclaiming to them "Thus saith the Lord." No listener ever forgot that Address, and among all the noble utterances of the speaker it may be questioned if one ever contained more truth in language more like that of immediate inspiration. . . .

Let us next call to the witness stand that other Cambridge boy whom we have already noted in the audience — the reckless, irreverent "Jamie" Lowell of 1837; sober enough now, when he gives his testimony, and it is the testimony, you will remember, of one of the few genuine critics whom America has produced:

The Puritan revolt had made us ecclesiastically and the Revolution politically independent, but we were socially and intellectually moored to English thought,

till Emerson cut the cable and gave us a chance at the
dangers and glories of blue water. No man young
enough to have felt it can forget or cease to be grateful
for the mental and moral *nudge* which he received from
the writings of his high-minded and brave-spirited
countryman. . . . His oration before the Phi Beta
Kappa Society at Cambridge, some thirty years ago,
was an event without any former parallel in our literary annals, a scene to be always treasured in the memory for its picturesqueness and its inspiration. What
crowded and breathless aisles, what windows cluster-
ing with eager heads, what enthusiasm of approval,
what grim silence of foregone dissent! It was our Yankee version of a lecture by Abélard, our Harvard parallel to the last public appearances of Schelling. . . .

Finally, lest you may think that the mere spell
of the orator's spoken word charmed such hearers
as Holmes and Lowell into an unreasoning disciple-
ship, listen to an opinion from across the water,
by a Scotchman who called no man, save Goethe,
master, and who read Emerson's speech in the
vast solitude of London town. Thomas Carlyle
wrote:

My friend! You know not what you have done for
me there. It was long decades of years that I heard
nothing but the infinite jangling and jabbering, and
inarticulate twittering and screeching, and my soul had
sunk down sorrowful, and said there is no articulate
speaking then any more, and thou art solitary among
stranger-creatures? and lo, out of the West comes a

clear utterance, clearly recognizable as a *man's* voice, and I *have* a kinsman and brother: God be thanked for it! I could have *wept* to read that speech; the clear high melody of it went tingling through my heart; I said to my wife, "There, woman!" She read; and returned, and charges me to return for answer, "that there has been nothing met with like it since Schiller went silent." My brave Emerson! And all this has been lying silent, quite tranquil in him, these seven years, and the "vociferous platitude," dinning his ears on all sides, and he quietly answering no word; and a whole world of Thought has silently built itself in these calm depths, and, the day being come, says quite softly, as if it were a common thing, "Yes, I *am* here too." Miss Martineau tells me, "Some say it is inspired, some say it is mad." Exactly so; no *say* could be suitabler. But for you, my dear friend, I say and pray heartily: may God grant you strength; for you have a *fearful* work to do! Fearful I call it; and yet it is great, and the greatest.

IV

MANY readers still imagine that Emerson's address had the advantage of a new theme. It did not. His subject, "The American Scholar," had been a conventional theme of Phi Beta Kappa orations ever since he was a boy. The records of the Harvard Chapter prove this fact, beyond dispute. In 1809, for example, the eloquent Dr. J. S. Buckminster, of Boston, had spoken on the "Dangers and Duties of Men of Letters"; an admirable moralistic discussion of the infirmities and temptations of the scholastic life, closing with a plea for increased endowments for Harvard. That was his solution of the difficulty!

In 1815, William Tudor, the editor of the newly founded "North American Review," had discussed the "subjects which America would furnish for future poets." This was a favorite topic for Tudor and his associate Walter Channing in the early volumes of the "North American"; and the burden of their argument was that the remedy for American deficiencies lay in a more vigorous exertion of our own minds.

In 1818, at the end of Emerson's Freshman year, Edward Tyrrel Channing, then commencing his long and fruitful career as a Harvard teacher of rhetoric, took for his Phi Beta Kappa theme, "Independence in Literary Pursuits."

In 1822, William J. Spooner, addressing the Society on "The Prospects of American Literature," admitted that all our literature, up to that date, was an English literature, and yet claimed that our literary destiny was to be as independent of England's as was our political and moral destiny. America, he maintains, has already given proofs of "the unconquerable mind"; now, "let our writers learn to think for themselves." Yet Mr. Spooner's peroration, like Dr. Buckminster's, emphasizes the necessity of enlarging the means of education and of raising the standards of scholarship — the old appeal, you will perceive, to Harvard men.

In 1824 came Edward Everett's oration, delivered in the presence of Lafayette and dedicated to him, on "The Peculiar Motives to Intellectual Exertion in America." Those of you to whom Everett's name has not become as shadowy as the names of Tudor and Buckminster will still read this speech with admiration. He uses the very words, "American scholar"; he pleads nobly for popular institutions, for "the manifold brotherhood which unites and will unite the growing millions of America." He sees in vision the vast populations of the Mississippi and Missouri valleys, waiting to be stirred and inspired by the American idea; and his peroration is not a plea for endowments for Harvard, but a welcome to Lafayette. Thus the years come and go with the Harvard Chapter, but the orators pound imperturbably away on the same note! In 1831, it is James T. Austin, on "The Character and Duties of Educated Men." In 1835, we have Judge Theophilus Parsons, "On the Duties of Educated Men in a Republic" — and an excellent standpat speech it is: pleading for the sovereignty of Truth, the sacredness of Law, the security of Property;

and President Wayland, of Brown University, the orator of 1836, made much the same plea under another title. In fact, such discussions of the duties and opportunities of the American Scholar were not confined to academic occasions. In 1831, Dr. William Ellery Channing had printed in the "Christian Examiner" his famous article on "National Literature." "In an age of great intellectual activity," he maintains, "we rely chiefly for intellectual excitement and enjoyment on foreign minds; nor is our own mind felt abroad. . . . We believe that a literature springing up in this new soil would bear new fruits. . . . Juster and profounder views of man may be expected here than elsewhere. In Europe political and artificial distinctions have, more or less, triumphed over and obscured our common nature. . . . Man is not hidden from us by so many disguises as in the Old World. . . ." Yet, as a means toward securing this new and native literature, Dr. Channing recommends "to our educated men a more extensive acquaintance with the intellectual labors of Continental Europe. Our reading is confined too much to English books, and especially to the more recent publications of Great Britain." Quickened by this contact with the Continental mind, power will pass increasingly, not into the hands of government, but into the hands of those who think and write. Thomas Carlyle, in that very year, was dreaming the same flattering dream.

You will thus perceive that when the Reverend R. W. Emerson announced in 1837 that his subject was to be "The American Scholar," the Cambridge audience could settle back comfortably in their seats, knowing pretty well what was coming — as you and I do when we listen to a Christmas or an Easter sermon. And I do not need to add that the comfortable Cambridge audience guessed wrong.

V

WHAT was it, after all, that Emerson said, upon his hackneyed theme? What was it that puzzled the elders, and entranced the youth, and sowed the seeds of division? At the Phi Beta Kappa dinner in University Hall, following the exercises in the church — a dinner too Bacchanalian, alas, for the taste of Brother John Pierce — Emerson was toasted in these words: "Mr. President, I suppose you all know where the orator came from; and I suppose all know what he said. I give you — the Spirit of Concord — *it makes us all of one mind.*" The pun was clever enough — as Phi Beta Kappa dinners go — but the well-meant compliment went very wide of the truth. Far from making them all of one mind, the man from

Concord had sowed discord — and Emerson, at least, knew it. At the Phi Beta Kappa dinner of the next year, he is aware, his Journal tells us, of the "averted faces," and the aversion dated from this very 31st of August, 1837 — it had only ripened by the summer of 1838 and the "Divinity School Address." What had he really uttered in this speech, which was no loving-cup, but a sword?

He had begun with decorous sentences, quiet and clear as the daylight. His very subject, he admits, is prescribed by the occasion. But before one knows it, he is making his first distinction, namely, that Man, in being divided into Men, has suffered, has become a thing — a farmer, let us say, instead of Man on the farm. Now the Scholar should be *Man Thinking*, not a mere thinker, or, still worse, the parrot of other men's thinking. What are the influences which the scholar receives?

There are three main influences: Nature, the Past — typified by Books — and Action.

First, then, Nature. "Every day, the sun; and, after sunset, Night and her stars. Ever the winds blow; ever the grass grows." But the scholar must ask what all this means. What *is* Nature? And then comes the puzzling Emersonian answer, already expressed in that little blue-covered un-

102

sold book of the year before: Nature is the opposite of the soul, answering to it part for part.
(I can fancy Brother John Pierce looking at his
watch. Ten minutes gone, and is this nonsense
about Nature what we came into the meeting-
house to hear?)

But the orator, after these cryptic paragraphs
about Nature, is already touching the second
influence upon the spirit of the scholar — namely,
the Past, or, let us say for convenience, Books.
(I imagine that Brother Pierce looks relieved.
Books? He has been hearing Phi Beta Kappa
talk about books for forty years. It is a safe subject. And yet what is it that the minister from
Concord seems to be saying now?) The theory of
books is noble, but each age must write its own
books. It is the act of creation that is sacred, not
the record. The poet chanting was felt to be a
divine man: henceforth the chant is divine also.
Instantly the book becomes noxious; the guide is
a tyrant, though colleges are built on it. (Can he
mean the Bible, wonders Professor Ware? Yes,
Professor Ware, he does mean the Bible, and he
will say so in your own Divinity School upon the
invitation of your own students, on the fifteenth
of July next! Listen to him as he goes on!) The
one thing in the world, of value, is the active soul.
The book, the college, the institution of any kind,

stop with some past utterance of genius. This is good, say they — let us hold by this. *They pin me down*. They look backward and not forward. Books are for the scholar's idle times. They serve us best when they aim, not to drill, but to create — when they set the hearts of youth on flame. (I should like to watch Professor Ned Channing's sarcastic face, as Waldo Emerson proclaims this doctrine: Waldo Emerson, who had proved himself in college neither drillable nor inflammable!)

But the imperturbable orator of the day has now reached the third section of his address — a plea for Action. Remember that we are in the golden and serious age of American Rhetoric, and do not smile when Emerson argues that action enriches the scholar's vocabulary! It is pearls and rubies to his discourse! Life is our dictionary. But action is after all better than books. Character is higher than intellect. Thinking is a partial act. The scholar loses no hour which the man lives. Labor is sacred. There is virtue yet in the hoe and the spade even in unlearned hands. (I catch grave young Henry Thoreau smiling a little as Mr. Emerson utters this wholesome New England doctrine of manual labor; — for he has watched the minister trying to spade his new Concord garden, and making but a sorry job of it!)

It remains, concludes the speaker, to say something of the scholar's duties. They may all be comprised in self-trust. Let him not quit his belief that a pop-gun is a pop-gun, though the ancient and honorable of the earth affirm it to be the crack of doom. Let him be free and brave. The world is still fluid, still alive. *Men* count — not "the mass" — "the herd." The private life is the true kingdom. Act for yourself: the man has never lived that can feed us ever. (Professor Ware — stout old war-horse — pricks up his ears again!) But now the orator is sweeping on to his climax: This age of Revolution in which we are living is a very good age. Accept it: embrace the common, the familiar, the low. Burns and Wordsworth and Carlyle are right. Give me insight into to-day, and you may have the antique and future worlds. The important thing is the *single person. The man is all*.

Then follows the wonderful peroration, which you would never forgive me for not quoting word for word:

. . . Mr. President and Gentlemen, this confidence in the unsearched might of man belongs, by all motives, by all prophecy, by all preparation, to the American Scholar. We have listened too long to the courtly muses of Europe. The spirit of the American freeman is already suspected to be timid, imitative, tame:

Public and private avarice make the air we breathe thick and fat. The scholar is decent, indolent, complaisant. See already the tragic consequence. The mind of this country, taught to aim at low objects, eats upon itself. There is no work for any but the decorous and the complaisant. Young men of the fairest promise, who begin life upon our shores, inflated by the mountain winds, shined upon by all the stars of God, find the earth below not in unison with these, but are hindered from action by the disgust which the principles on which business is managed inspire, and turn drudges, or die of disgust, some of them suicides. What is the remedy? They did not yet see, and thousands of young men as hopeful now crowding to the barriers for the career do not yet see, that if the single man plant himself indomitably on his instincts, and there abide, the huge world will come round to him. Patience — patience; with the shades of all the good and great for company; and for solace the perspective of your own infinite life; and for work the study and the communication of principles, the making those instincts prevalent, the conversion of the world. Is it not the chief disgrace in the world, not to be an unit; — not to be reckoned one character; — not to yield that peculiar fruit which each man was created to bear, but to be reckoned in the gross, in the hundred, or the thousand, of the party, the section, to which we belong; and our opinion predicted geographically, as the north, or the south? Not so, brothers and friends — please God, ours shall not be so. We will walk on our own feet; we will work with our own hands; we will speak our own minds. The study of letters shall be no longer a name for pity, for doubt, and for sensual indulgence.

The dread of man and the love of man shall be a wall of defense and a wreath of joy around all. A nation of men will for the first time exist, because each believes himself inspired by the Divine Soul which also inspires all men.

VI

THAT, then, is what Emerson said, eighty-six years ago. What do we think of it? We know what Brother Pierce thought of it, and what was the verdict of Holmes and Lowell and Carlyle. I have amused myself — though I may have wearied you — by intimating what this hearer and that, among the long-vanished audience, may have surmised or hoped or resolved in his own heart, as those beautiful cadences ceased at last, and the great hour was over. I might tell what was said in the newspapers and in the Reviews, and how the entire edition of the address was sold out in one month, whereas it took thirteen years to sell the first five hundred copies of the orator's book on "Nature." Yet all such evidence, interesting as it may be to one's antiquarian curiosity, does not fully explain the meaning or the power of Emerson's address.

The words of Emerson's speech are still legible upon the printed page, but how small a portion of any speech are the mere words! Boys declaim them in school, "meek young men in libraries"

study the sources, literary historians endeavor to
reconstruct the time and place of utterance. Yet
the magic has fled with the magical hour, and the
words seem only the garments of a soul that has
escaped. The chemical formula for a great speech
seems simple enough, but it is mysterious, like all
simple things; it is *a Man plus the atmosphere of a
given epoch*. The speech falls flat if it be uttered
a year, a month, a day earlier or later than its
appointed hour. See young Wendell Phillips
fighting his way to the platform of Faneuil Hall
on December 8th of that very year, 1837, to
defend the memory of Lovejoy from the attack of
the Attorney-General of Massachusetts. It is
now or never for what Phillips has to say, and
Phillips knows it. See him forty-four years later,
in Sanders Theater, as the Phi Beta Kappa orator of 1881, defending Russian Nihilism; some of
us can remember the tense excitement of the
American public in that hour over the question of
freedom in Russia. Almost no one in Sanders
Theater knew what Phillips was to say. Official
Harvard, as always, distrusted him. His flashing
eloquence, that noon, was the electric discharge,
through him, of forces greater than the orator. If
you will read that address of 1881 to-day, you cannot withhold your admiration for the cunning art
of the consummate craftsman. The right words

are all there in their right places. But the spell is
broken; "the image of the God is gone."

Now, it is a part of the genius and the glory of
Emerson that his spoken words have the accent
of literature. Their specific form is, indeed, shaped
by the heat and pressure of an occasion. But their
substance is perdurable. His phrases are final
phrases. His aim is Truth, and not mere eloquence. He has, indeed, learned the art of rhetoric
from Everett and Webster, but he has also
learned, by watching them, to distrust rhetoric —
to keep it in its place. He would like to win his
immediate audience, no doubt, but he is forever
saying to himself, as Lincoln said of his debates
with Douglas in 1858, "there is bigger game than
this." Lincoln's ultimate object was to justify
the fundamental principles of free government.
Emerson's goal was the Truth that sets men free.
His words are literature because the Truth that he
perceived could be revealed only through Beauty.
The revealing phrase is lovely, and the uncovered
face of Truth is lovelier still. As Emerson discourses of Nature and Books and Action, he lays
bare his own mind, as an athlete strips himself for
the race. Exquisite perception of external beauty,
ripened wisdom, high courage — these were the
man, and by their perfect expression of the man's
qualities Emerson's addresses win their place as

literature. We read them to-day as we read Montaigne or Bacon, as something forever alive.

I remarked to a friend the other day that I was trying to imagine what Emerson would say if he had to make his Phi Beta Kappa speech over again in the present hour. "If Emerson were living to-day," was the reply, "he would be a very different Emerson." In one sense, of course, my friend was right. If Emerson had been born seventy-five years later, he would have read Tolstoy and Ibsen, he would have studied under William James, and he would use a somewhat different vocabulary. It is likely that he would have written no Journals. He would have missed the discipline and support of the Lyceum audiences. But he would certainly be giving Lowell Institute lectures, as of old, and writing for the "Atlantic Monthly," and lunching with the Saturday Club. It is certain that he would be making Phi Beta Kappa speeches, and I think we may be allowed to guess what he would say. He would still, I believe, have a message for you and me, a message for our academic communities, and a counsel of perfection for the United States.

To the private person he would announce, with the old serenity: "The sun shines to-day also" — "and, after sunset, Night and her stars." In uttering this gospel of Nature he would use new terms, for his mind would have been fascinated by the new discoveries. But while the illustrations would be novel, he would still assert the universality of Law. He would still say: Books are good, but the living soul is better. "Do not teach me out of Leibnitz and Schelling, and I shall find it all out myself." He would still preach to us the gospel of the will, or, in William James's phrase, "the will to believe." "When you renounce your early visions, then dies the man in you." Be a unit. In this whirring social machinery of the twentieth century, in this over-organized, sentimentalized, and easily stampeded age, possess your own soul. By and by the snowstorm of illusions will cease, and you will be left alone with the moral laws of the universe, you alone and they alone. When that supreme hour comes, meet it without fear.

Emerson's message to the academic community would have, I think, a note of yearning. The historic Emerson always wished to be one of us. There was no time in his long career, his biographer says, when he would not gladly have accepted a professorship of rhetoric in any college. If he were of our generation, but still, as of old, outside of our own immediate circle, would he not say: "O you who are cramped in costly buildings, clogged with routine, preoccupied with administrative ma-

chinery, how can you see the sun whether it be
shining? Where is your free hour for Night and her
stars? You are learned in bibliographies, expert in
card catalogues, masters of a thousand specialties.
You are documented, certificated, sophisticated.
But have you the old eager reverence for the great
books? And where, by the way, are your own
books? From these thousands of American
colleges and universities, how many vital, creative
books are born? The university of Walden Pond
had 'Whim' written above its doorposts, but it
bred literature. There was once a type of productive scholar who may be described as 'he that
scattereth, and yet increaseth,' but your amazing
and multifarious activity, is not much of it wast-
age rather than growth? Simplify! Coördinate!
Find yourselves, and then lift up your hearts!"

And finally I am sure that the spirit of Emerson,
if he were revisiting this "great sensual avaricious
America," as the historic Emerson once called
it, would have a message for the United States
in this hour of cowardice, disillusionment, and in-
hibition. Unless Emerson came back from the
under-world with a changed soul, he would assert
the supremacy of moral obligations. He would
perceive, as in his lifetime, that a "diffidence in
the soul was creeping over the American mind."
But he would shame that diffidence. He would

rally the distrustful. Can we not hear once more his clear and quiet voice: The gods are forever in their places: first, Righteousness, Justice, and Liberty, and after these, Fellowship and Peace. The Law holds. The foundations of human society are moral foundations. They cannot be shaken, even though whole empires should lose their senses and debauch their souls and go toppling down. Be steady. "This time, like all times, is a very good one, if we but know what to do with it." Behold the Law: "God is, not was; He speaketh, not spake." The world is very wide, very strange, it terrifies us, it seems plunging from its orbit. But it cannot plunge from its orbit; that was fixed before the foundation of the world. Patience — patience. Our earth is whirling on its way from God and to God, and the law of its being is the same law of obedience and of faith which is written in the heart of the obscurest scholar.

EMERSON'S SAVINGS BANK

This Book is my Savings Bank
EMERSON'S *Journals*, III, 246

I

THE phrase used by Emerson to describe his
life-long persistence in keeping a diary is char-
acteristically modest. His mental habits, like
his physical endowments, necessitated thrift; a
rigid economy and investment of his resources.
The college notebooks of the boy of seventeen,
and the last jottings of the practiced rhetorician,
whose memory for words had begun pathetically
to lapse, are alike dominated by the impulse to
conserve for future need. At the beginning of his
academic training he sets down in his Journal a
list of poetical phrases "for use." He composes
paragraphs "in the manner of Chateaubriand,"
loving for a while, like Stevenson, to play the
sedulous ape. He quotes resonant passages from
Edward Everett; constructs boyish discourses
on the Drama, on Reason, on Benevolence; endeavors to analyze himself and his associates; but
all this is chiefly the elaborate exercise of an ambitious boy, a rhetorician by inheritance and

training, who feels himself destined to sway his contemporaries through public speech.

As he grows older, and enters upon and then terminates his brief career as a minister, the character of the writing changes a little. There are fewer of the futile exercises in mere composition — like a golfer's preliminary swings at an imaginary ball. The experiences which he records are sometimes grimly real, though they are still set down "for use." As the years go by, there is an increasing tendency to record mere mood — in the manner of Amiel — but there is also a rich deposit of local and provincial fact: racy sayings of Concord folk, shrewd judgments upon contemporaries, accounts of walks with Hawthorne, Ellery Channing, and Thoreau, and of conversations with "Margaret" and Alcott. More significant still are the deliberately garnered thoughts of Emerson himself, gleaned from saunterings in the upland pastures or from the wind-blown eddies upon Walden Pond. They are the dispersed meditations of a man of the rarest poetic and philosophic temper, who was not always capable of complete functioning either as poet or philosopher. He knew this well enough, and it was one reason for the careful gathering of every possible material — wood heaped for a bonfire that might one day blaze.

The multitudinous manuscript volumes of the Journals were carefully indexed as to topics, by Emerson's own hand. It was a kind of perpetual balancing of his bank-books. From them he drew the substance of his public lectures, and these became in turn — somewhat stripped of anecdote and other platform adornments — the Essays as we know them. Sometimes, too, the first rough draft of a poem — like "Each and All," "The Two Rivers," "Days" — appears in the Journal, although such efforts were more commonly inscribed in a separate verse-book, to await elaboration. The manuscript volumes occasionally contain prosaic accounts of expenses, income from lecturing, charitable contributions, and miscellaneous almanac information which have not been reproduced by the editors. But they have had nothing to conceal, and the ten stout volumes which now complete their labors are essential to a full realization of Emerson's character. More perfectly than he could have imagined, his diaries have thus become his Bank. His patient thrift is justified.

II

THE quality of the writing, from first to last, is one of sustained excellence. Like Emerson's penmanship, it varied but little during his long

116

career of authorship, and even when his sentences were intended for no eye but his own, he wrought them carefully and felicitously. Perhaps it would be more accurate to say that he composed habitually, not for the eye, but for the ear. The oral impulse was strong in this descendant of eloquent sires, the admiring auditor of Everett and Webster, the unwearied searcher and practitioner of the mysteries of the spoken word. Yet even in his college days, which fell in our brazen age of Oratory, there was singularly little buncombe in the young Emerson's style. He was captivated by the extravagant declamation of some of his Southern classmates, and forty years afterwards used to recite specimens of it for the amusement of his children, but his own ear remained unspoiled. Like his master, Montaigne, he was always talking on paper as to the first man he met, but it was the talk of an observer, a quester, a poet — not the orotund banalities of the "spellbinder." There is no doubt a certain oral diffuseness upon many pages of the Journals. Some of his spiritual experiences were overwritten. These Solitaries and Recluses, imprisoned in their temperament, as Emerson said of himself, will still be talking! But Emerson's Journal is less repetitious than Thoreau's, and it never grows really garrulous. The rhapsodical passages of nature-description have that perfection of "tone" which Emerson thought more essential to poetry than the presence of fine lines, and the more introspective pages are often marked by a startling incisiveness and spiritual passion. The great words of the Phi Beta Kappa Oration and of the Divinity School Address vibrate in the Journal long before they thrilled the ear of the actual hearers. In the crises of his professional life no less than in these crucial public utterances the Journals prove that Emerson crossed his real bridges long before he came to the overt act of crossing. Hence the tranquillity with which he notes the acceptance of his resignation by the Second Church, and the "averted faces" at the Harvard Commencement of 1838. The actual event presented itself to him as a twice-told tale: the precedent spiritual drama is written in the Journals. Familiarity with Emerson's published writings thus heightens one's sense of the freshness and reality of his private diary. The editors have done wisely to reprint here the first draft of many a well-known passage of the Essays, believing the unelaborated words to be no less golden, and perceiving that the cadences have "that other harmony" of unpremeditated talk.

Selections from the multifarious topics touched upon by an alert and brooding mind during a long lifetime must of necessity be arbitrary. Perhaps the student of Emerson is first arrested by the presence, in the earlier volumes of the Journals, of the word "sin." That word, and the aspect of evil which it denotes, can scarcely be discovered in the Essays. But the young Emerson finds — or has been trained to suspect — "a huge and disproportionate abundance of *evil* on earth." (I, 246.) "Love has an empire in the world, but Fear has an empire also." (I, 295.) In a long and fascinating passage of self-assessment (I, 367), he proposes to devote his nights and days "to the service of God and the War against Sin." The call to the Second Church came just as he had become aware of his love for Ellen Tucker: "This happiness awakens in me a certain awe: I know my imperfections: I know my ill-deserts; and the beauty of God makes me feel my own sinfulness the more. . . . Will God forgive me my sins, and aid me to deserve this gift of his mercy?" (II, 261.)

A new stage in Emerson's development is marked by his ingenious endeavor to reconcile the acquired vocabulary of Transcendentalism — which proclaimed the supremacy of the "Reason" over the "Understanding" — with the traditional vocabulary of his forbears. "Jesus Christ was a minister of the pure Reason. The beatitudes of the Sermon on the Mount are all utterances of the mind contemning the phenomenal world. . . . The Understanding can make nothing of it. 'Tis all nonsense. The reason affirms its absolute verity. . . . St. Paul marks the distinction by the terms natural man and spiritual man. When Novalis says 'It is the instinct of the Understanding to counteract the Reason,' he only translates into a scientific formula the sentence of St. Paul, 'The carnal mind is enmity against God.'" (III, 237.)

When Emerson wrote that passage he had already abandoned the ministry, and within a year, in 1834, he was confiding to his diary: "If I were called upon to charge a young minister, I would say, 'Beware of Tradition'" (III, 420), and a few pages later: "The Teacher that I look for . . . will not occupy himself by laboriously reanimating a historical religion, but in bringing men to God by showing them that He is, not was, and speaks, not spoke." (III, 434.) Four years afterward, those words became the dynamite of the Divinity School Address.

Traces of Emerson's revolt against historical Christianity are clear enough throughout the Journals. Sometimes they take the form of rebellion against "official goodness" and the restraints of the ancestral profession. Again, it is the moral constitution of man which seems to the prophet to be weakened by reliance upon dogma: "Christ's great Defeat is hitherto the highest fact we have, ... but we demand Victory." (VI, 189.) The final volume gives a whimsical and delightfully boyish turn to this lifelong restlessness against compulsion: "The Bible wears black cloth. It comes with a certain official claim against which the mind revolts. The book has its own nobilities — might well be charming, if it was left simply on its merits, as the others; but this 'you must' — 'it is your duty,' repels. 'Tis like the introduction of martial law into Concord. If you should dot our farms with picket lines, and I could not go or come across lots without a pass, I should resist, or else emigrate. If Concord were as beautiful as Paradise, it would be detestable at once." (X, 101.)

Yet the note of loyalty to the representatives of the old order, like Mary Moody Emerson and Dr. Ripley, is eloquently sounded upon many a page, and the virtues of this disappearing type are seen to be rooted in their "unpainted churches, strict platforms, and sad offices." This recalcitrant son of the Puritans remained a Puritan in every fiber of the body and of the memory; it was only his questing mind which went voyaging toward new worlds. As with Hawthorne, Longfellow, Whittier, and Lowell, accomplished antiquarians all, his passionate attachment to the older New England survived every change of creed and of philosophy.

III

THIS fidelity to the spirit of the soil gives the Journals their extraordinary interest as a local document. Judge Sewall's Diary is equally veracious in reporting certain aspects of the New England temperament, but Emerson's capacity for detachment, as well as his experiences in European and Western travel, give his pictures of the everyday life a perspective such as Sewall could not compass. The "cold gentleness" of New England women in church; "the iron-gray deacon and the wearisome prayer rich with the diction of ages"; what perfect phrases are these! With what delight, too, did this fastidious scholar record the savory sayings of his unlettered neighbors! There are relatively few entries dealing with the more intimate life of his own household, although the editors have preserved the poignant sentences written after the deaths of his brothers Edward and Charles and of his son Waldo. But of objective depiction of the villagers of Concord there is no lack, and the humor and tartness of the portraiture will surprise many readers who know Emerson only through his poems and essays.

Thoreau's Journal, it is true, gives us more meticulous facts about Concord; more exact measurements of acreage and weather, more fauna and flora; but even Thoreau does not surpass Emerson in conveying the very aspect of the hour and the place. Thoreau himself, and Alcott and Ellery Channing, are sketched in many moods and attitudes. Alcott is by turns an Olympian, a "tedious archangel," a "pail without bottom," until we reach the climax in Emerson's plaintive "I do not want any more such persons to exist." Such is the Journal's tardy revenge upon one of the notable devastators of the day.

National figures, likewise, cross from time to time the decorous local stage. Edward Everett and Daniel Webster, Garrison, John Brown, and Lincoln are viewed with eyes only less "portrait-eating, portrait-painting" than Carlyle's. During each of his three visits to Europe, Emerson had met on intimate footing some of the most distinguished personages of his day. He knew a man when he saw him, and he employed inflexible standards of moral measurement. The whole story of Webster's dominance in New England, and of his tragic alienation from his constituents after 1850, may be gathered from the successive descriptions of him in the Journals. At first we read of his "awful charms," for Emerson had heard him deliver the famous eulogy upon Adams and Jefferson. After the reply to Hayne, Webster becomes to Emerson a synonym of "the beauty and dignity of principles." The first word of dispraise is in 1835, when Webster seems to be concealing his opinion of slavery. In 1841: "I saw Webster on the street; but he was changed since I saw him last — black as a thunder-cloud, and careworn. . . . The canker-worms have crawled to the topmost bough of the wild elm, and swing down from that." Early in 1843 Emerson is still capable of exact, passionless description of the colossus; but later in that year he notes: "Daniel Webster is a great man with a small ambition" — the verdict which Hawthorne had already uttered in "The Great Stone Face." After the speech of March 7, 1850, Webster seemed to Emerson a mere traitor to Liberty: "Every drop of his blood has eyes that look downward." As for the Fugitive Slave Law, enacted through Webster's influence, Emerson enters this oath in his Journal (VIII, 236): "I will not obey it, by God." Looking across the hazy water from Plymouth to Marshfield on the day of Webster's death in 1852, he mourns the passing of the "completest man" since Napoleon, yet this did not alter the terms of his terrific indictment of the dead statesman in his New York speech of 1854.

In fact, the eighth and ninth volumes of the Journals, covering the critical national period of 1849 to 1863, reveal an Emerson startled out of his preoccupation with his own thoughts and alive to every issue of citizenship. He was, indeed, the perfect villager in his natural response to every claim of wont and neighborhood, but in the dark days he learned to feel nationally when other men were still arguing in the terms of their own section. To read his Journals now, when his views have been tested by the event, is to perceive the clearness and soundness of his tone upon the great public questions. His frequent lecturing trips to the Mississippi and beyond, journeys whose discomforts and humors were duly set down in his diary, helped him, no doubt, to think continentally.

It is impossible here to make more than an allusion to one of the most delightful aspects of the Journals, namely, their judgments upon books and authors. They reinforce the impression conveyed by the Essays as to the range and inconsecutiveness of Emerson's reading. That he should ever have held himself faithfully to the task of reading Goethe straight through in the original German is an amazing proof of his respect for Carlyle's opinion. He knew the "complete works" of few writers except Montaigne, Shakespeare, and

Plutarch. He preferred, as everybody has surmised and as the Journals now demonstrate, to
saunter and angle in one author after another,
and to say his own say about fragments: confess-
ing good luck with Rabelais to-day and poor luck
to-morrow, as a fisherman does with his favorite
stream. Emerson's judgments of literary art —
as of all the arts of expression except oratory —
were often fallible enough. "The poor Pickwick
stuff" was not for him; neither was Jane Austen
nor Hawthorne. Shelley "is never a poet." Yet
he catches the odor of Alfred Tennyson's "musky
verses" by 1838; and he was early and always
faithful to Wordsworth, though he shared Jeffrey's
astounding incomprehension of the finest lines in
the "Ode to Duty." More significant, however,
than the oddness or the justice of any single verdict of this inveterate skimmer of books is the
perfect candor and sense of security with which
he deposits his opinion in the Bank.

IV

MANY readers of the Journals, no doubt, will not
concern themselves primarily with the phases of
Emerson's development, with his judgments upon
men and books and public events, or with his
daguerreotypes of the daily life of Concord. They
will seek, rather, an escape from the daily life —

whether it be Emerson's or their own — into
those regions of ecstasy of which the Poems and
the Essays long ago gave glimpses. Such readers
will not be disappointed. All the old magic is
here. The day-long reverie in a sunny hollow of
the woods at Mount Auburn (III, 270), when the
man of thirty-one, then without a profession,
"heeded no more what minute or hour our Massachusetts clocks might indicate" and "saw only
the noble earth on which I was born," is scarcely
to be matched save in a few passages of Sénancour
and Amiel and in a few lines of Andrew Marvell.
The morning meditation in the newly furnished
house in Concord (IV, 335) is the Emersonian
reply to one of the ultimate questions: "I said
when I awoke, After some more sleepings and
wakings I shall lie on this mattress sick; then,
dead; and through my gay entry they will carry
these bones. Where shall I be then? I lifted my
head and beheld the spotless orange light of the
morning beaming up from the dark hills into the
wide universe." The mysteries of the night are
in this invocation to the Earth Spirit (VI, 347):
"Earth Spirit, living, a black river like that
swarthy stream which rushes through the human
body is thy nature, demoniacal, warm, fruitful, sad,
nocturnal." Yet the daytime magic is the more
characteristic of the man: "The sky is the daily

bread of the eyes.... No crowding: boundless, cheerful, and strong." "The sum of life ought to be valuable when the fractions and particles are so sweet." Or, finally, take this enchanting affirmation, written, apparently, after reading Balzac's story (VI, 273): "*Le Peau d'Ane*. You *can* do two things at a time; and when you have got your pockets full of chestnuts, and say I have lost my half-hour, behold you have got something besides, for the tops of the Silver Mountains of the White Island loomed up whilst you stood under the tree, and glittered for an instant; therefore there is no *peau de chagrin*."

V

FOR those who do not care for these enchantments of Merlin, but who welcome fresh material for the valuation of an historical and literary personage, it remains to be said that the Journals offer a new basis for the critical assessment of our most distinguished man of letters. The requisite biographical, physiological, and psychological data are here. The temperamental inconsistencies, so often hinted at in the Essays, are set down in plain figures in this bank account. Its analysis of the author's body and mind and environment proceeds steadily from youth to age. Emerson makes open confession of the impossibility of his

achieving a philosophical reconciliation of the op-
positions which he perceives. The Journals, like
the Essays, are full of paradoxes, but they furnish
more keys of fact wherewith to unlock their par-
ables. The volumes will prove to be the natural
corrective of partial and distorted views of Emerson. (The main outlines of his towering personality
are, it is true, unaffected by the revelations of his
private diary.) He remains the austere, benignant
figure so familiar to his countrymen: a radiant,
serene vision against the morning or the evening
sky. Some of the angles are curiously sharpened,
as one looks at him through the Journals, but the
figure as a whole is softened; it becomes richer and
more human; the granite and the cloud are suffused with life. The next generation of readers
will utilize the Journals for a new criticism of
Emerson.

JAMES RUSSELL LOWELL [1]

I

Two Harvard men, teachers of English in the
University of North Carolina, have recently published a new kind of textbook for undergraduates.
Abandoning the conventional survey of literary
types and the examination of literary history in
the narrow sense of those words, they present a
programme of ideas, the dominant ideas of successive epochs in the life of England and America.
They direct the attention of the young student,
not so much to canons of art as to noteworthy ex-
pressions of communal thought and feeling, to the
problems of self-government, of noble discipline,
of ordered liberty. The title of this book is "The
Great Tradition." The fundamental idealism of
the Anglo-Saxon race is illustrated by passages
from Bacon and Raleigh, Spenser and Shakespeare.
But William Bradford, as well as Cromwell and
Milton, is chosen to represent the seventeenth-
century struggle for faith and freedom. In the
eighteenth century, Washington and Jefferson

[1] An address delivered at the exercises held by the Cambridge
Historical Society in Sanders Theater, February 22, 1919, to commemorate the centenary of Lowell's birth.

and Thomas Paine appear side by side with
Burke and Burns and Wordsworth. Shelley and
Byron, Tennyson and Carlyle are here of course,
but with them are John Stuart Mill and John
Bright and John Morley. There are passages
from Webster and Emerson, from Lowell and
Walt Whitman and Lincoln, and finally, from the
eloquent lips of living men — from Lloyd George
and Arthur Balfour and Viscount Grey and President Wilson — there are pleas for international
honor and international justice and for a commonwealth of free nations.

It is a magnificent story, this record of Anglo-
Saxon idealism during four hundred years. The
six or seven hundred pages of the book which I
have mentioned are, indeed, rich in purely literary material; in the illustration of the temper of
historic periods; in the exhibition of changes in
language and in literary forms. The lover of sheer
beauty in words, the analyzer of literary types,
the student of biography, find here ample material for their special investigations. But the stress
is laid, not so much upon the quality of individual
genius as upon the political and moral instincts
of the English-speaking races, their long fight for
liberty and democracy, their endeavor to establish
the terms upon which men may live together in
society. And precisely here, I take it, is the

significance of the pages which Professors Green-
law and Hanford assign to James Russell Lowell.
The man whom we commemorate to-night played
his part in the evolution which has transformed
the Elizabethan Englishman into the twentieth-
century American. Lowell was an inheritor and
an enricher of the Great Tradition.

This does not mean that he did not know
whether he was American or English. He wrote
in 1866 of certain Englishmen: "They seem to
forget that more than half the people of the North
have roots, as I have, that run down more than
two hundred years deep into this new-world soil
— that we have not a thought nor a hope that is
not American." In 1876, when his political independence made him the target of criticism,
he replied indignantly: "These fellows have no
notion what love of country means. It is in my
very blood and bones. If I am not an American,
who ever was?"

It remains true, nevertheless, that Lowell's life
and his best writing are keyed to that instinct of
personal discipline and civic responsibility which
characterized the seventeenth-century emigrants
from England. These successors of Roger As-
cham and Thomas Elyot and Philip Sidney were
Puritanic, moralistic, practical; and with their
"faith in God, faith in man and faith in work"

they built an empire. Lowell's own mind, like Franklin's, like Lincoln's, had a shrewd sense of what concerns the common interests of all. The inscription beneath his bust on the exterior of Massachusetts Hall runs as follows: "Patriot, scholar, orator, poet, public servant." Those words begin and end upon that civic note which is heard in all of Lowell's greater utterances. It has been the dominant note of much of the American writing that has endured. And it is by virtue of this note, touched so passionately, so nobly, throughout a long life, that Lowell belongs to the elect company of public souls.

No doubt we have had in this country distinguished practitioners of literature who have stood mainly or wholly outside the line of the Great Tradition. They drew their inspiration elsewhere. Poe, for example, is not of the company; Hawthorne in his lonelier moods is scarcely of the company. In purely literary fame, these names may be held to outrank the name of James Russell Lowell, as Emerson outranks him, of course, in range of vision, Longfellow in craftsmanship, and Walt Whitman in sheer power of emotion and of phrase. But it happens that Lowell stands with both Emerson and Whitman in the very center of that group of poets and prose-men who have been inspired by the American idea. They were all, as we say proudly nowadays, "in the service," and the particular rank they may have chanced to win is a relatively insignificant question, except to critics and historians.

II

THE centenary of the birth of a writer who reached threescore and ten is usually ill-timed for a proper perspective of his work. A generation has elapsed since his death. Fashions have changed; writers, like bits of old furniture, have had time to "go out" and not time enough to come in again. George Eliot and Ruskin, for instance, whose centenaries fall in this year, suffer the dark reproach of having been "Victorians." The centenaries of Hawthorne and Longfellow and Whittier were celebrated at a period of comparative indifference to their significance. But if the present moment is still too near to Lowell's lifetime to afford a desirable literary perspective, a moral touchstone of his worth is close at hand. In this hour of heightened national consciousness, when we are all absorbed with the part which the English-speaking races are playing in the service of the world, we may surely ask whether Lowell's mind kept faith with his blood and with his citizenship, or whether, like many a creator of exotic, hybrid beauty, he remained an alien in the spiritual commonwealth, a homeless, masterless man.

No one needs to speak in Cambridge of Lowell's devotion to the community in which he was born and in which he had the good fortune to die. In some of his most delightful pages he has recorded his affection for it. Yonder in the alcoves of Harvard Hall, then the College Library, he discovered many an author unrepresented among his father's books at Elmwood. In University Hall he attended chapel — occasionally. In the open space between Hollis and Holden he read his "Commemoration Ode." He wrote to President Hill in 1863: "Something ought to be done about the trees in the Yard." He loved the place. It was here in Sanders Theater that he pronounced his memorable address at the two hundred and fiftieth anniversary of the founding of the College — an address rich in historic background, and not without solicitude for the future of his favorite humanistic studies — a solicitude, some will think, only too well justified. "Cambridge at all times is full of ghosts," said Emerson. But no ghost from the past, flitting along the Old Road from Elmwood to the Yard, and haunting the bleak lecture-rooms where it had recited as a careless boy and taught wearily as a man, could wear a more quizzical and friendly aspect than Lowell's.

He commonly spoke of his life as a professor with whimsical disparagement, as Henry Adams wrote of his own teaching with a somewhat cynical disparagement. But the fact is that both of these self-depreciating New Englanders were stimulating and valuable teachers. From his happily idle boyhood to the close of his fruitful career, Lowell's loyalty to Cambridge and Harvard was unalterable. Other tastes changed after wider experience with the world. He even preferred, at last, the English blackbird to the American bobolink, but the Harvard Quinquennial Catalogue never lost its savor, and in the full tide of his social success in London he still thought that the society he had enjoyed at the Saturday Club was the best society in the world. To deracinate Lowell was impossible, and it was for this very reason that he became so serviceable an international personage. "You knew where he stood. It was not for nothing that his roots ran down two hundred years deep. He was the incarnation of his native soil.

Lowell has recently been described, together with Whittier, Emerson, and others, as an "English provincial poet — in the sense that America was still a literary province of the mother country." To this amazing statement one can only rejoin that if "The Biglow Papers," the "Harvard Commemoration Ode," "Under the Old Elm," the "Fourth of July Ode," and the Agassiz elegy are English provincial poetry, most of us need a new map and a new vocabulary. Of both series of "Biglow Papers" we may surely exclaim, as did Quintilian concerning early Roman satire, "This is wholly ours." It is true that Lowell, like every young poet of his generation, had steeped himself in Spenser and the Elizabethans. They were his literary ancestors by as indisputable an inheritance as a Masefield or a Kipling could claim. He had been brought up to revere Pope. Then he surrendered to Wordsworth and Keats and Shelley, and his earlier verses, like the early work of Tennyson, are full of echoes of other men's music. It is also true that in spite of his cleverness in versifying, or perhaps because of it, he usually showed little inventiveness in shaping new poetic patterns. His tastes were conservative. He lacked that restless technical curiosity which spurred Poe and Whitman to experiment with new forms. But Lowell revealed early extraordinary gifts of improvisation, retaining the old tunes of English verse as the basis of his own strains of unpremeditated art. He wrote "A Fable for Critics" faster than he could have written it in prose. "Sir Launfal" was composed in two days, the "Commemoration Ode" in one.

III

It was this facile, copious, enthusiastic poet, not yet thirty, who grew hot over the Mexican War and poured forth his indignation in an unforgettable political satire such as no English provincial poet could possibly have written. What a weapon he had, and how it flashed in his hand, gleaming with wit and humor and irony, edged with scorn, and weighted with two hundred years of Puritan tradition concerning right and wrong! For that, after all, was the secret of its success. Great satire must have a standard; and Lowell revealed his in the very first number and in one line:

> "'Taint your eppylets an' feathers
> *Make the thing a grain more right.*"

Some readers to-day dislike the Yankee dialect of these verses. Some think Lowell struck too hard; but they forget Grant's characterization of the Mexican War as "one of the most unjust ever waged by a stronger against a weaker nation." There are critics who think the First Series of "Biglow Papers" too sectional; an exhibition of New England's ancient tendency toward nullification of the national will. No doubt Lowell underestimated the real strength of the advocates of national expansion at any cost. Parson Wilbur thought, you remember, that

"All this big talk of our destinies
Is half on it ign'ance an' t'other half rum."

Neither ignorance nor rum was responsible for the invasion of Belgium; but at least one can say that the political philosophy which justifies forcible annexation of territory is taught to-day in fewer universities than were teaching it up to 1914. Poets are apt to have the last word, even in politics.

IV

THE war with Mexico was only an episode in the expansion of the slave power; the fundamental test of American institutions came in the War for the Union. Here again Lowell touched the heart of the great issue. The Second Series of "Biglow Papers" is more uneven than the First. There is less humor and more of whimsicality. But the dialogue between "the Moniment and the Bridge," "Jonathan to John," and above all, the tenth number, "Mr. Hosea Biglow to the Editor of the Atlantic Monthly," show the full sweep of Lowell's power. Here are pride of country, passion of personal sorrow, tenderness, idyllic beauty, magic of word and phrase.

Never again, save in passages of the memorial odes written after the war, was Lowell more completely the poet. For it is well known that his was a divided nature, so variously endowed that complete integration was difficult, and that the circumstances of his career prevented that steady concentration of power which poetry demands. She is proverbially the most jealous of mistresses, and Lowell could not render a constant allegiance. At thirty his friends thought of him, rightly enough, as primarily a poet: but in the next fifteen years he had become a professor, had devoted long periods to study in Europe, had published prose essays, had turned editor, first of the "Atlantic," then of the "North American Review," and was writing political articles that guided public opinion in the North. To use a phrase then beginning to come into general use, he was now a "man of letters." But during the Civil War, I believe he thought of himself as simply a citizen of the Union. His general reputation, won in many fields, gave weight to what he wrote as a publicist. His editorials were one more evidence of the central pull of the Great Tradition: it steadied his judgment, clarified his vision, kept his rudder true.

Lowell's political papers during this period, although now little read, have been praised by Mr. James Ford Rhodes as an exact estimate of public sentiment, as voicing in energetic diction the mass of the common people of the North. Lincoln wrote to thank him for one of them, adding, "I fear I am not quite worthy of all which is therein kindly said of me personally." Luckily Lincoln never saw an earlier letter in which Lowell thought that "an ounce of Frémont is worth a pound of long Abraham." The fact is that Lowell, like most men of the "Brahmin caste," came slowly to a recognition of Lincoln's true quality. Motley, watching events from Vienna, had a better perspective than Boston then afforded. Even Mr. Norton, Lowell's dear friend and associate upon the "North American Review," thought in 1862 that the President was timid, vacillating, and secretive, and, what now seems a queerer judgment still, that he wrote very poor English. But if the editors of the "North American" showed a typical Anglo-Saxon reluctance in yielding to the spell of a new political leadership, Lowell made full amends for it in that superb Lincoln strophe now inserted in the "Commemoration Ode," afterthought though it was, and not read at the celebration.

In this poem and in the various Centennial Odes composed ten years later, Lowell found an instrument exactly suited to his temperament and his technique. Loose in structure, copious in diction, swarming with imagery, these Odes gave ample scope for Lowell's swift gush of patriotic fervor, for the afflatus of the improviser, steadied by reverence for America's historic past. To a generation beginning to lose its taste for commemorative oratory, the Odes gave — and still give — the thrill of patriotic eloquence which Everett and Webster had communicated in the memorial epoch of 1826. The forms change, the function never dies.

The dozen years following the Civil War were also the period of Lowell's greatest productiveness in prose. Tethered as he was to the duties of his professorship, and growling humorously over them, he managed, nevertheless, to put together volume after volume of essays that added greatly to his reputation, both here and in England. For it should be remembered that the honorary degrees of D.C.L. from Oxford and LL.D. from Cambridge were bestowed upon Lowell in 1873 and 1874; long before any one had thought of him as Minister to England, and only a little more than ten years after he had printed his indignant lines about

"The old J. B.
A-crowdin' you and me."

J. B. seemed to like them! A part of Lowell's full harvest of prose sprang from that habit of enormous reading which he had indulged since boyhood. He liked to think of himself as "one of the last of the great readers"; and though he was not that, of course, there was, nevertheless, something of the seventeenth-century tradition in his gluttony of books. The very sight and touch and smell of them were one of his pieties. He had written from Elmwood in 1861: "I am back again in the place I love best. I am sitting in my old garret, at my old desk, smoking my old pipe and loving my old friends." That is the way book-lovers still picture Lowell — the Lowell of the "Letters" — and, though it is only a half-length portrait of him, it is not a false one. He drew upon his ripe stock of reading for his college lectures, and from the lectures, in turn, came many of the essays. Wide as the reading was in various languages, it was mainly in the field of "belles-lettres." Lowell had little or no interest in science or philosophy. Upon one side of his complex nature he was simply a book-man like Charles Lamb, and like Lamb he was tempted to think that books about subjects that did not interest him were not really books at all.

V

RECENT critics have seemed somewhat disturbed over Lowell's scholarship. He once said of Longfellow: "Mr. Longfellow is not a scholar in the German sense of the word — that is to say, he is no pedant; but he certainly is a scholar in another and perhaps a higher sense. I mean in range of acquirement and the flavor that comes with it." Those words might have been written of himself. It is sixty-five years since Lowell was appointed to his professorship at Harvard, and during this long period erudition has not been idle here. It is quite possible that the University possesses to-day a better Dante scholar than Lowell, a better scholar in Old French, a better Chaucer scholar, a better Shakespeare scholar. But it is certain that if our Division of Modern Languages were called upon to produce a volume of essays matching in human interest one of Lowell's volumes drawn from these various fields, we should be obliged, first, to organize a syndicate, and, second, to accept defeat with as good grace as possible.

Contemporary critics have also betrayed a certain concern for some aspects of Lowell's criticism. Is it always penetrating, they ask? Did he think his critical problems through? Did he have a body of doctrine, a general thesis to maintain? Did he always keep to the business in hand? Candor compels the admission that he often had no thesis to maintain: he invented them as he went along. Sometimes he was a mere guesser, not a clairvoyant. We have had only one Coleridge. Lowell's essay on Wordsworth is not as illuminating as Walter Pater's. The essay on Gray is not as well ordered as Arnold's. The essay on Thoreau is quite as unsatisfactory as Stevenson's. It is true that the famous longer essays on Dante, Chaucer, Spenser, Shakespeare, Dryden, Milton, are full of irrelevant matter, of facile delightful talk which often leads nowhere in particular. It is true, finally, that a deeper interest in philosophy and science might have made Lowell's criticism more fruitful; that he blazed no new paths in critical method; that he overlooked many of the significant literary movements of his own time in his own country.

But when one has said all this, even as brilliantly as Mr. Brownell has phrased it, one has failed to answer the pertinent question: "Why, in spite of these defects, were Lowell's essays read with such pleasure by so many intelligent persons on both sides of the Atlantic, and why are they read still?" The answer is to be found in the whole tradition of the English bookish essay, from the first appearance of Florio's translation of Montaigne down to the present hour. That tradition has always welcomed copious, well-informed, enthusiastic, disorderly, and affectionate talk about books. It demands gusto rather than strict method, discursiveness rather than concision, abundance of matter rather than mere neatness of design. "Here is God's plenty!" cried Dryden in

his old age, as he opened once more his beloved
Chaucer; and in Lowell's essays there is surely
"God's plenty" for a book-lover. Every one
praises "My Garden Acquaintance," "A Good
Word for Winter," "On a Certain Condescension
in Foreigners," as perfect types of the English
familiar essay. But all of Lowell's essays are dis-
cursive and familiar. They are to be measured,
not by the standards of modern French criticism
— which is admittedly more deft, more delicate,
more logical than ours — but by the unchartered
freedom which the English-speaking races have
desired in their conversations about old authors
for three hundred years. After all,

"There are nine-and-sixty ways of constructing tribal lays
[. And every single one of them is right."

Lowell, like the rest of us, is to be tested by what
he had, not by what he lacked.

VI

His reputation as a talker about books and men
was greatly enhanced by the addresses delivered
during his service as Minister to England. Henry
James once described Lowell's career in London
as a tribute to the dominion of style. It was even
more a triumph of character, but the style of these
addresses is undeniable. Upon countless public

occasions the American Minister was called upon
to say the fitting word; and he deserved the quaint
praise which Thomas Benton bestowed upon
Chief Justice Marshall, as "a gentleman of
finished breeding, of winning and prepossessing
talk, and just as much mind as the occasion re-
quired him to show." I cannot think that Lowell
spoke any better when unveiling a bust in West-
minster Abbey than he did at the Academy dinners in Ashfield, Massachusetts, where he had
Mr. Curtis and Mr. Norton to set the pace; he
was always adequate, always witty and wise; and
some of the addresses in England, notably the one
on "Democracy" given in Birmingham in 1884,
may fairly be called epoch-making in their good
fortune of explaining America to Europe. Lowell
had his annoyances like all ambassadors; there
were dull dinners as well as pleasant ones, there
were professional Irishmen to be placated, solemn
dispatches to be sent to Washington. Yet, like
Mr. Phelps and Mr. Bayard and Mr. Choate and
the lamented Walter Page in later years, this
gentleman, untrained in professional diplomacy,
accomplished an enduring work. Without a trace
of the conventional "hands across the sea"
banality, without either subservience or jingoism,
he helped teach the two nations mutual respect
and confidence, and thirty years later, when

England and America essayed a common task in safeguarding civilization, that old anchor held.

VII

THIS cumulative quality of Lowell's achievement is impressive, as one reviews his career. His most thoughtful, though not his most eloquent verse, his richest vein of letter-writing, his most influential addresses to the public, came toward the close of his life. Precocious as was his gift for expression, and versatile and brilliant as had been his productiveness in the 1848 era, he was true to his Anglo-Saxon stock in being more effective at seventy than he had been at thirty. He was one of the men who die learning and who therefore are scarcely thought of as dying at all. I am not sure that we may not say of him to-day, as Thoreau said of John Brown, "He is more alive than ever he was." Certainly the type of Americanism which Lowell represented has grown steadily more interesting to the European world, and has revealed itself increasingly as a factor to be reckoned with in the world of the future. Always responsive to his environment, always ready to advance, he faced the new political issues at the close of the century with the same courage and sagacity that had marked his conduct in the eighteen-forties. You remember his answer to

Guizot's question: "How long do you think the American Republic will endure?" "So long," replied Lowell, "as the ideas of its founders continue to be dominant"; and he added that by "ideas" he meant "the traditions of their race in government and morals." Yet the conservatism revealed in this reply was blended with audacity — the inherited audacity of the pioneer. No line of Lowell's has been more often quoted in this hall than the line about the futility of attempting to open the "Future's portal with the Past's blood-rusted key." Those words were written in 1844. And here, in a sentence written forty-two years afterward, is a description of organized human society which voices the precise hope of forward-looking minds in Europe and America at this very hour: "The basis of all society is the putting of the force of all at the disposal of all, by means of some arrangement assented to by all, for the protection of all, and this under certain prescribed forms." Like Jefferson, like Lincoln, like Theodore Roosevelt at his noblest, Lowell dared to use the word "all."

Such men are not forgotten. As long as June days come and the bobolink's song "runs down, a brook of laughter, through the air"; as long as a few scholars are content to sit in the old garret with the old books, and close the books, at times, to think of old friends; as long as the memory of brave boys makes the "eyes cloud up for rain"; as long as Americans still cry in their hearts, "O beautiful, my country!" the name of James Russell Lowell will be remembered as the inheritor and enricher of a great tradition.

WOODROW WILSON AS A
MAN OF LETTERS [1]

SHORTLY after the close of Mr. Cleveland's second term as President, he delivered in Princeton, where he had taken his residence, a notable public address. It contained a powerful and indignant sentence about the recent refusal of the United States Senate to ratify the treaties of arbitration — treaties which had expressed, Mr. Cleveland declared, the plain wish of the people of the United States. Mr. Cleveland had few of the gifts and none of the arts of the orator, but that single massive, downright sentence, weighted with his whole character and vibrating with intense feeling, thrilled his audience as I have rarely seen an audience moved by any master of speech. It touched the imagination, like a glimpse of Hercules wielding his club. As the crowd moved slowly out of Alexander Hall, I remarked to a professor of theology: "What a sledgehammer of a sentence!"

"Exactly," said the theologian; "and it was just the weapon for a President. You know, you don't want to have a President of the United

[1] *The Century*, March, 1913.

States write with as fine a style as Woodrow
Wilson."

That was fifteen years ago. A good deal has
happened in the interval. Five years after the
delivery of Mr. Cleveland's speech, another great
audience in Alexander Hall listened with admiration and delight to Woodrow Wilson's inaugural
address as President of Princeton. Here was a
scholar, a favorite child of his alma mater, an
admitted master of style. In delicate and supple
phrase, with learning and logic and conviction,
with a profound sense of the obligations which the
cloistered college owes to the larger world, President Wilson announced the aims of his adminis-
tration. The representative Americans who were
present at that inaugural address were aware that
they were listening to one of the foremost of our
living men of letters, expounding with consummate
beauty of expression and transparent sincerity
of feeling his pattern and dream of an ideal university. But, curiously enough, and as one remembers words of evil omen, I recall the casual remark
of one of the guests of the university as the audience dispersed. He was an observant journalist.

"Very beautiful speech of Wilson's," he said,
"very noble; but over the heads of the two trustees
who sat in front of me."

I shall not debate the validity of that last

clause. Local opinion differed on this point, and the general public has refused to take any great interest in the fact itself or in its alleged consequences. But the two offhand judgments upon Woodrow Wilson's style which I have ventured to quote suggest a certain instinctive and widespread feeling that a master of words is not likely to be a master of things or of men; that the functions of a man of letters and of a president of a republic are so essentially different that recognized ability in the one calling may render its possessor suspect if he happen to be summoned by the people to perform the duties of their chief executive. It is interesting, therefore, to look closely at the equipment and performance of this brilliant talker and writer who has been called to the Presidency. Is Woodrow Wilson's way of talking and writing a fine accomplishment merely, like the skill of a piano-player who is no musician at heart; or is the whole man in this instance so thoroughly of one piece that his phrases reveal his actual personality? No answer to such a question will satisfy everybody. There will continue to be persons who believe that mastery over language is something external to a man's true character: that it is, to use the familiar image, a suit of clothes to be put on or off at pleasure, as if one could assume his good French or good English with his evening dress, though he speak but wretched French or English in his working hours. And there will always be that deeper skepticism which distinguishes between the fine talker and the fine doer, and distrusts the first because so much of the world's best work has been done by the "silent" men. These old suspicions that language is a disguise or a disqualification die hard.

Concerning one aspect of Woodrow Wilson's style there can be but little difference of opinion: he talks precisely as he writes and he writes as he talks. When M. Raymond Poincaré, a man of letters whose rise to the foremost political station affords a curious parallel to that of Woodrow Wilson, was admitted to the French Academy in 1909, his old teacher, M. Ernest Lavisse, after some delightful chaffing, paid this compliment to the new Academician: "Nous connaissons assez votre écriture pour que je puisse vous addresser ce compliment que vous parlez comme vous écrivez et que vous écrivez comme vous parlez. Mon très cher et regretté maître, Gaston Boissier, disait à ses élèves: 'Ne vous mettez pas dans l'état littéraire quand vous prenez la plume.' Vous ne vous mettez ni dans l'état littéraire, avant d'écrire, ni dans l'état oratoire avant de parler."[1]

[1] "Your style is sufficiently familiar to us to warrant my offering you this compliment: You speak as you write and you write as

Mr. Wilson surely has never needed to put himself into the literary state of mind as a preparation for writing, nor into the oratorical state of mind as a preparation for speaking. The mind and the style are the same throughout.

Such easy command over himself and his resources is, of course, the result of long discipline, and a discipline in which, from the beginning, oral utterance has had as important a part as written utterance. By inheritance, circumstance, and ambition, Woodrow Wilson has been a respecter of speech. A clergyman's son; a son, too, of that Virginia where oratory has always been held in honor; a lad who wrote with boyish humor on one of his earliest visiting-cards, "Thomas W. Wilson, U.S. Senator"; an eager college debater; a hater of slang and all slovenliness of phrase; a painstaking expositor of close legal and governmental reasoning in many varied classrooms; a platform speaker constantly in demand for a score of years preceding his campaign for the governorship of New Jersey, his skill and resourcefulness and steadiness in that singular compaign surprised nobody but his enemies. He had been training for it

you speak. My very dear and much-regretted master, Gaston Boissier, used to say to his students: 'Do not put yourselves in a literary frame of mind as soon as you take up the pen.' You do not put yourself in a literary frame of mind before writing, nor in an oratorical one before speaking."

from youth. With but an indifferent physical
equipment, he had won his rank by sheer persist-
ency of will, by patient thinking on public questions, by intensity of feeling. Back of that expository forefinger of the "schoolmaster" stood a
master of his subject, a debater who had been
winning debates all his life, a Scotch-Irishman
who had something of Jefferson's preference for a
"little rebellion now and then," and considerably
more than Jefferson's fondness for a fight.

His campaigning cleverness was distrusted
then, as it has been later, by some of his fellow
citizens whose wits work more slowly than his,
and whose social imagination is less flexible.
Many of his loyal supporters, even, have occasionally found his political utterances too vague;
luminous enough, but luminous with the suffused
light of sunlit haze. Precisely the same fault has
been found with many another "literary statesman"; with Gladstone preëminently, but also
with Disraeli, Balfour, Morley, Thiers, and
Poincaré. Oral utterance has its dangers, like
every other mode of human expression. But for
a man who is capable of profiting by its lessons, it
nevertheless affords one of the most valuable
schools of purely literary discipline. Words, even
when they are used primarily as weapons of controversy, remain wonderful things. It was the

discipline of oral utterance in frontier store and tavern, and upon the circuit and the stump, which forged and tempered Lincoln's speech into a marvelous instrument for literature. To lift story-telling and legal exposition and party argument to the higher levels of literature there are needed, no doubt, other elements than mere dexterous command of the spoken word. There must be the pressure and glow of great ideas and strong emotions, as in Burke, or a transcendent cause, such as that which chastened and ennobled the unselfish lips of Lincoln, before there can be that inexplicable chemistry which changes words into something more than words, which transforms mere prose into a strange but enduring kind of poetry. Such transformations are mysteries, after all is said. The political orator can merely perfect himself to the uttermost of his gifts and opportunities. The rest lies in character, and in the unforeseen. Yet no unpartisan person, I should suppose, can fail to perceive in Woodrow Wilson's public utterances the qualities of mind and the magical power over spoken syllables which are the basis of all oratory that lives.

This achievement, notable as it is, has been steadily accompanied by a purely literary discipline. He began as an essayist, and it is as an essayist that his most distinguished writing has been done. His style matured very early, and he has been heard to complain whimsically that he wrote as well in college as he could twenty-five years later. He had been graduated but six years when he published his "Congressional Government," a brilliant study which in the stout seventeenth-century days would have been called an essay. By that one book he gained his reputation. His "Division and Reunion" may also, without disparagement, be termed a long historical essay, a clear, swiftly moving, dispassionately just narrative of known facts and tendencies rather than the laborious setting forth of material discovered by first-hand investigation. The magazine papers on "George Washington" likewise made a delightful book rather than a substantial enlargement of our knowledge of the subject. "The History of the American People" was an ambitious undertaking for a college professor engaged in many other tasks. It was rapidly written, and the circumstances of its composition precluded that long absorption of the author with his "sources," that year-in and year-out imaginative living with the past which has entered into the very texture of the epoch-making histories. It is full of admirable characterizations, of skillful summary of events, and it has given pleasure to multitudes of readers. But the professional historians, who are possibly too much inclined to insist on the closed shop and to resent the intrusion of men of letters into their factory, seem to think that "The History of the American People" is somehow not a "contribution."

Perhaps this is merely the old antagonism between the quarrymen and the architect. In Mr. Wilson's "Century" article entitled, "The Truth of the Matter," he has set forth his views upon the writing of history.[1] Obviously, what interests him primarily is the art of the historian rather than the task of the investigator. "The investigator must display his materials, but the historian must convey his impressions. . . . The historian needs an imagination quite as much as he needs scholarship, and consummate literary art as much as candor and common honesty." Academic historians are afraid of this doctrine, which has recently been preached to them, nevertheless, by Colonel Roosevelt in his address on "History and Literature." Mr. Roosevelt and Mr. Wilson agree in substance. The Colonel's essay is the more vigorous, and is packed with allusions drawn from amazingly wide reading. It sounds as though it had been dictated to a stenographer with immense

[1] See *The Century* for September, 1895: "On the Writing of History, with a glance at the methods of Macaulay, Gibbon, Carlyle, and Green."

zest. The professor's essay is not dictated, but composed; it is more varied, more subtle, more distinguished: but the views of the two men are essentially the same, and the unionized historical "investigators" can extract but little comfort from either of them.

I believe that Woodrow Wilson's best writing has not yet been put on paper. But the next best, surely — and it is better than most men's best — is in such essays as "The Truth of the Matter," "On Being Human," and "Mere Literature." The "Atlantic" essays on "Reconstruction" and "Mr. Cleveland as President," together with the earlier papers on Burke, Bagehot, and "The Author Himself," may well keep them company. Foremost among his instructors in thought and style stands Burke, whose influence may be perceived upon almost every page of Mr. Wilson's books, as in nearly every paragraph of his addresses. Next comes Walter Bagehot. In Mr. Wilson's earlier essays the phrase, "as Mr. Bagehot says," occurs as frequently as that admiring, "as Mr. Everett says," in the early Journals of Emerson. Augustine Birrell has had a hand in the business, too; and Lamb and Wordsworth and Boswell's "Johnson." The intellectual influences that have really counted in Woodrow Wilson's development are almost purely English and

American. Plato and the Roman consuls have
left scarcely a trace, and modern France and Germany quite as little. His reading, aside from the
technical treatises on law, government, and
politics which have been incidental to his professional work, has been well within the limits of
the "gentleman's library." But it has been a
thoughtful, brooding, vital kind of reading.

His style is undeniably "bookish," as Lamb and
Stevenson are bookish. At times there are quaint,
innocent affectations in it, like the "'Twas,"
"'Tis," "'Twould" which decorate the pages of
Hazlitt and the elder essayists. As compared with
the unconscious, pure style of John Fiske, or the
veracious sentences of Mr. James Ford Rhodes, it
seems to be just a trifle aware of itself, knowing what "sets my genius best," as Alan Breck
Stewart said of his favorite sword-play. And
"Alan Breck" himself was not more gay and alert
than are the best passages of Woodrow Wilson.
It is witty, high-spirited, exhilarating writing.
It has the Southern virtues, schooled by stern self-
discipline into an avoidance of typical Southern
faults; it has sentiment without sentimentality,
ease without diffuseness, eloquence without declamation. With all of its delicate, bookish overtones, it remains essentially the style of a speaker.
It addresses itself to the ear rather than to the

eye, and its occasional over-anxieties are the
solicitude of a well-bred converser, fearing to fail
to please, or to be misinterpreted.

There is one other quality of Mr. Wilson's style,
curiously interesting now that he has won, by
means of politics, a national audience. "It be-
hooves all minor authors," he wrote long ago, "to
realize the possibility of their being discovered
some day and exposed to the general scrutiny."
This has been precisely his own fortune. But
from the first there has been a sort of spaciousness
in his pages, a consciousness of wide backgrounds
and far horizons. It is betrayed in one of his
favorite metaphors — the wind blowing over
great spaces. "To speak of national affairs is to
give hint of great forces and of movements blown
upon by all the airs of the wide continent." "His
world [Sir Henry Maine's] seemed to be kept always clear of mists and clouds, as if it were blown
through with steady trade winds, which brought
with them not only pure airs, but also the harmonious sounds and the abiding fragrance of the great
round world." There is the same image of the
blowing wind, and I think not a little of unconscious self-portraiture in his picture of Henry
Clay: "His nature [Clay's] was of the West,
blown through with quick winds of ardor and
aggression, a bit reckless and defiant; but his art

was of the East, and ready with soft placating phrases, reminiscent of old and reverenced ideals, thoughtful of compromise and accommodation." It is the quick, imaginative movement of Woodrow Wilson's own mind, blown through as it is with "ardor and aggression," and yet "thoughtful of compromise," which is now forced to bear the scrutiny of "pitiless publicity," and to be analyzed by his countrymen with admiration or with concern.

Mr. Wilson's mind and style may coarsen in the rough battles of the Presidency. Such deterioration is not unknown, and undeniably the coarser style has a certain effectiveness for the vast democratic audience. Here is a typical example of it, taken from a decade characterized, as the last decade has been characterized, by party faction, reckless demagogic leadership, "trial by newspaper," and the gleeful shoutings of the mob. It is the famous "No. 45" of John Wilkes's "North Briton," issued on the 23d of April, 1763, and sentenced to be burned by the common hangman as an "infamous and seditious libel." It declared:

This week has given the public the most abandoned instance of ministerial effrontery ever attempted to be imposed on mankind. The minister's speech of last Tuesday is not to be paralleled in the annals of the country. I am in doubt whether the imposition is

163

greater on the sovereign or on the nation. Every friend of his country must lament that a prince of so many great and amiable qualities, whom England truly reveres, can be brought to give the sanction of his sacred name to the most odious measures and to the most unjustifiable public declarations, from a throne ever renowned for truth, honour, and unsullied virtue.

Clever Jack Wilkes, with that "Every-friend-of-his-country" style! And here is a telegram in this very morning's newspaper (January 5, 1913): "I am confident that I express the feelings of every decent American citizen when I say that I am outraged and indignant beyond measure at the infamy that has been perpetrated in Idaho." It is a style that pleases some of the people all of the time.

A humorist, himself in high position, is understood to have affirmed recently that Governors and Presidents must needs grow emphatic and profane in office. Possibly the explanation may be found in the remark of a New England spinster to a blameless kinsman of hers who confessed that he was more sorely tempted to say "damn" at forty than he had been at twenty-five. "Perhaps," she suggested tartly, "you are beginning to see things in their true light." And yet there has been at least one clear-sighted and disillusioned President whose mind and style grew steadily finer and not coarser, whom vast responsibilities made more patient, more considerate of differences of opinion and policy. Let Lincoln's victory in the great ordeal be a happy augury for his latest successor.

Woodrow Wilson is the first professional man of letters to become President of the United States. No man who has entered the White House since Lincoln has been better equipped by character and training to ennoble and refine the tone of public utterance.

POSTSCRIPT

(1923)

THE foregoing pages were published in March, 1913 — a date which now seems nearly as remote as the Trojan War. Yet I am obstinate enough to reprint the essay. There is danger, of course, as well as pleasure, in saying "I told you so," but I cannot resist pointing out that my prophecy of ten years ago — "Woodrow Wilson's best writing has not yet been put on paper" — gives me to-day some quiet critical satisfaction. I believed that he had it in him to write great things, and now there are millions of readers who echo John Burroughs's verdict: "All his war papers are like messages written in the sky. They get the attention of the entire world, and deserve it."

No one in 1913 could possibly have anticipated that a World War would provide this immense audience for President Wilson's utterances. Nor could one anticipate the intense political and personal feeling in the United States which created a hostile or admiring attitude toward everything which the President might say. John Burroughs himself had begun by thinking Wilson a "coiner of phrases"; it was only after 1917 that he spoke of "messages written in the sky." A well-known friend of Burroughs, and a master of epithet, characterized the President as a "Byzantine logothete." A Federal Judge, trained at Harvard, pronounced Wilson's style to be that of a "floor-walker"; — a judgment which reminds me somehow of a letter about Lincoln written by Charles Eliot Norton in 1862. "We think the President's style poorer than ever," said this fastidious New-Englander. Yet Norton must have read the Lincoln-Douglas debates, and the Cooper Union speech, and Lincoln's First Inaugural Address! No one in Lincoln's lifetime, however, devoted a whole book to an analysis of his English. William Bayard Hale performed this service — or disservice — for Wilson in 1920 in "The Story of a Style." It is a melancholy story, if Mr. Hale is to be trusted. His list of Wilson's "aristocratic affectations," "learned addictions," "symbolisms," and "phonetic phenomena" is readable, exhaustive, and often acutely drawn. But his general conclusions, which are to the effect that Mr. Wilson "never entertained an original idea on any subject," that "his writings are marked conspicuously and obstinately by some of the signs often associated with sub-normal intellectuation," and that "vagueness and reiteration, symbolism and incantation I take to be the chief secrets of Mr. Wilson's verbal power," manage to suggest that poor Woodrow Wilson ought to be in some sort of an asylum. Perhaps an asylum for floor-walkers.

I cannot help remembering that twenty years ago, before any political and personal rancors were associated with his name, the editors of the "Century," "Harper's," and "Atlantic" were vying with one another to secure articles by Woodrow Wilson. The editors thought then that no American writer except John Fiske possessed such clearness, grace, and force of style for magazine purposes. Did they know their business, or did they not? Is it best to turn skeptic, and to deny that anybody knows whether he or any man really writes well? Is this whole matter of style so personal that we are all perpetually fooled? If we dislike a man or his ideas or his political policies, can we possibly form a dispassionate judgment upon his "clearness, force, and elegance," or upon any other conventional tests of rhetorical excellence?

There is the case of Thomas Jefferson, whom Mr. Wilson resembles in so many ways. Jefferson had a peculiar personality, a disconcerting mental habit, a political prescience, a prophetic fervor and exaltation which seemed and still seems insincere to those who cannot share it; and this personality must be viewed through the refraction of an atmosphere thick with political passions of every shade. What New England Federalist could possibly estimate Jefferson rightly? By the way, has any writer on style, from Aristotle to Mr. J. Middleton Murry, tried to explain the inexplicable psychology of American politics and its influence upon American literary judgments?

Mr. Hale was quite right — whatever may have been his motive — in indicating certain faults in Mr. Wilson's style. There are defects in the style of every great writer. Even Newman, keen and supple controversialist as he was, developed a written style admirable as an expression of his own mental operations, but bound to seem "Jesuitical" in the eyes of Newman's Protestant contemporaries. It was so essentially subtle as to be regarded with distrust by the typical Anglo-Saxon

168

reader. And Mr. Wilson's style has likewise its subtleties. It is also a bit redundant at times, a bit repetitious, a bit tinged with Stevensonian over-elaboration. Stevenson confesses to having "loved the art of words." So may Mr. Wilson, and in fact every man who desires to write well. But neither Stevenson nor any one else in our time has had his phrases quoted against him so pitilessly as President Wilson. Some of the most intelligent of his fellow citizens grew apoplectic with rage over the famous unlucky phrases: the "too proud to fight," the "peace without victory," and "the objects of all the belligerents the same." They were too angry to be reminded of the connections and the purpose with which such clauses were spoken or written. If you asked them to read the entire paragraph or the entire speech before passing judgment upon an isolated phrase, you were considered as little better than a pro-German. It all goes to prove that under the present conditions of newspaper publicity no man in high office can hope to have his words weighed carefully or his utterances measured as a whole. In times of excitement the public will never remember an entire address. It will catch at single phrases and use them without reason or imagination or mercy. Burke and Webster had opponents with some sense of sportsmanship, but the age of sportsmanship in American politics has disappeared.

I think it is hopeless, therefore, to look for any general agreement upon Woodrow Wilson's mastery of language until our generation has passed away. But surely a publicist who once desired "to play for the verdict of mankind" can afford to wait for it. And while we are waiting, I will hazard the opinion that President Wilson's addresses of January 22, 1917, April 2, 1917, and January 8, 1918, are such examples of great writing as can scarcely be matched in the long history of English political prose.

LITERARY CRITICISM IN AMERICAN
PERIODICALS

I

"THE literary man in this country has no critic."
These words appear in Emerson's Journal for
October 23, 1836. Emerson was then thirty-three.
He had received the conventional academic and
professional training of a New-Englander of that
day. He had deliberately broken with the church
of his ancestors, had settled in Concord to follow
the career of a man of letters, and had just published his first book. Other entries in his diary for
1836 give pungent expression to his solicitude for
the status of American art and letters. He exam-
ines, as so many cultivated Americans were just
then examining, the obstacles to the intellectual
life of a half-developed country, not yet emerged
from its position of colonial dependency upon
England as regards the things of the mind. It is
evident that he is already preparing, though quite
unconsciously as yet, his Phi Beta Kappa Address
of 1837 on "The American Scholar." He does not
whine over the unsatisfactory state of American
literature: he is simply analyzing, with that tone
of shrewd, dispassionate assurance which he

never lost, the causes of our deficiency. One of them is the absence of intellectual standards: "The literary man in this country has no critic."

Did Emerson tell the truth? And if he told the truth for the year 1836, is his charge still true after the lapse of more than three quarters of a century? These are the questions which I shall attempt to discuss in a survey of the nature and tendencies of literary criticism in American periodicals. For if literary standards are really existent in the minds of the reading public, if criticism is actually functioning, the merest glance at the periodicals of a country, in any epoch, will reveal the fact.

Even before Emerson's day, Dennie's "Portfolio" and other journals had experimented with native criticism. Emerson was himself the son of a literary critic; and "The Monthly Anthology" which the Reverend William Emerson had helped to found in Boston was welcomed by Dennie's "Portfolio" in 1805 in words that give a vivid description of the literary situation:

So unfrequent in America is the intercourse between men of letters, so sullen is the genius of republicanism, so wide is our waste of territory, so narrow our prejudices, so local our interests, so humble our means either of receiving or imparting knowledge, that we have but little of that *esprit de corps* which characterizes the

Literati of Europe. Our men of letters scarcely ever act in concert; each unconscious and often careless of what another is doing, proceeds sullenly alone, and a Magazine, or even works less ephemeral, may be projected and executed in Boston, of whose authors and whose objects an inquirer at Philadelphia or Baltimore, may be profoundly ignorant.

That passage was written just ten years before the founding of the "North American Review" in Boston, in 1815. William Tudor, Jr., the editor of the "Review," and his associate, Dr. Walter Channing, confessed in the first and second volumes of the new periodical that America had no national language and no literature except Indian literature; that it was still colonial, deficient in literary enterprise and in genuine intellectual courage. But it is significant to note the difference in spirit between the editors of the "Monthly Anthology" and those of the "North American." The earlier men took England as their model. They declared:

We know of no American language, that is not Indian, and feel no inclination to resort to the Choctaws, the Chickasaws, the Cherokees, and the Tuscaroras for literary instruction. Whilst we speak and write the English language, we are satisfied to be guided in our use of that language by approved English writers, by which we shall guard against modern foppery and provincial impurities.

173

Excellent young men! But Tudor and Walter Channing were looking forward and not backward. The remedy for American deficiences, said William Ellery Channing, must lie in a vigorous exertion of our own minds.

Even a casual examination of American periodicals during the score of years preceding 1836 will reveal the fact that many cultivated and able men were attempting to write literary criticism; and, as Professor Cairns pointed out in 1898, this movement was by no means confined to those Eastern cities which were most immediately in touch with European books and with European standards of culture. To be still more specific, and to select that very year, 1836, which I have taken as a convenient starting-point, suppose one turns the pages of the "Southern Literary Messenger." To its junior editor, a dark-eyed, bow-legged, taciturn, and somewhat difficult gentleman named Poe, was entrusted the task of reviewing the new books. He tore them open with restless energy, and tested their pages by a keener analysis than had hitherto been known upon this side of the Atlantic. He was only twenty-seven, but he was already a craftsman. Like the late Mr. W. P. Garrison, of "The Nation," he had his theories concerning the semicolon and the dash, and he expounded them with satisfaction and even with joy. Poe hated a clumsy sentence as the elder Garrison abhorred slavery, and he thought it a proper task for criticism to expose violations of English grammar and cruel abuse of the particles of speech. Yet out of the ninety-four books which he reviewed in nine months for the "Messenger," not more than three or four are actually flayed. In fact, the Poe of 1836 is surprisingly kind, and often complaisant: the flashing knife of Apollo is for the moment darkened in its sheath. But though Poe's good nature, in that year, may seem to us excessive, he nevertheless maintains a stern respect for what he calls "the determinate principles" of criticism. He anticipates and opposes that declaration of literary independence which Emerson was to draft, a year later, in the address on "The American Scholar." "We are becoming boisterous and arrogant," says Poe, "in the pride of a too speedily assumed literary freedom. We throw off, with the most presumptuous and unmeaning hauteur, all deference whatever to foreign opinion — we forget, in the true inflation of vanity, that the world is the true theater." Here he occupies precisely the same position which Dr. William Ellery Channing had taken in 1830, in recommending "to our educated men a more extensive acquaintance with the intellectual labors of continental Europe. Our reading is confined too much to English books, and especially to the more recent publications of Great Britain."

The most complete formulation of Poe's views upon periodical criticism is found, however, in his "Exordium" to the January number of "Graham's Magazine" in 1842 — the year, and the magazine, in which he wrote his famous criticism of Hawthorne's "Twice-Told Tales." Americans are beginning, Poe writes, "to inquire into the offices and provinces of criticism — to regard it more as an art based immovably in nature, less as a mere system of fluctuating and conventional dogmas. And, with the prevalence of these ideas, has arrived a distaste even to the home-dictation of the bookseller-*coteries*. If our editors are not as yet *all* independent of the will of a publisher, a majority scruple, at least, *to confess* a subservience." The British quarterly reviews, Poe continues, have degenerated under the practice of anonymous criticism. Originally "a review" "reviewed or surveyed the book whose title formed its text, and, giving an analysis of its contents, passed judgment upon its merits or defects" — an admirable statement, by the way, of the aim of so-called "judicial" criticism. The British journals, on the contrary, have allowed a general and diffuse essay upon the subject-matter of a publication to take the place of a review proper.

The French reviews, for example, which are *not* anonymous, are very different things, and preserve the unique spirit of true criticism. And what need we say of the Germans? — what of Winckelmann, of Novalis, of Schelling, of Goethe, of Augustus William, and of Frederick Schlegel? . . . Criticism is *not*, we think, an essay, nor a sermon, nor an oration, nor a chapter in history, nor a philosophical speculation, nor a prose-poem, nor an art-novel, nor a dialogue. In fact, it *can be* nothing in the world but — a criticism. . . . A book is written — and it is only *as the book* that we subject it to review. With the opinions of the work, considered otherwise than in their relation to the work itself, the critic has really nothing to do. It is his part simply to decide upon *the mode* in which these opinions are brought to bear.

I find this "Exordium" of Edgar Allan Poe, even in the condensed form in which I am obliged to present it, a refreshing bit of writing. I do not wish to raise the skeptical inquiry as to how much Winckelmann, Novalis, and Schelling he had really read, nor to ask, at the moment at least, whether his platform of criticism was broad enough for the shuffling feet of his great master Coleridge, broad enough for Sainte-Beuve and Arnold, for Brunetière and Anatole France, for Mr. Brownell and for Mr. Woodberry. It was at any rate broad enough for Poe, the most acute of our craftsman-critics, our most pathetically loyal disciple of the doctrine of "determinate principles." When Emerson wrote that "the literary man in this country has no critic" he must have forgotten, or, what is more likely, he had up to that time never heard of the "jingle-man" in Richmond.

By 1842, the date of the "Exordium" which I have just quoted, Emerson was himself writing book reviews for "The Dial," and for forty years thereafter he had leisure and opportunity to note the prevailing tone and tendency of American periodical criticism. He saw his associates upon "The Dial," Miss Margaret Fuller and George Ripley, join the literary staff of the New York "Tribune"; and his friend Charles A. Dana, the pietistic poet of Brook Farm, become the editor of the New York "Sun." Emerson contributed to the first number of the "Atlantic Monthly," a magazine which aimed from the beginning to elevate the standard of critical writing. He read the critical essays of his friends Lowell and Whipple, and watched the career of the rejuvenated "North American Review," under the direction of Lowell and Norton. He was an early reader of the New York "Nation." He lived long enough to see the first volumes of the Chicago "Dial." Only two months before his death he published his finely critical article on "The Superlative" in the "Century Magazine." He witnessed, in short,

before the close of his observant life in 1882, that
extraordinary development of daily, weekly, and
monthly journalism in America, which has deluged
the land with talk about everything, and inciden-
tally with talk about books.

II

WOULD Emerson have said at the end of his literary career, as he did at the beginning, that the
literary man in this country had no critic? It is
my impression that he would, although I cannot
prove it, and I admit that Emerson, like his proto-
type Montaigne, has occasionally a dismaying
trick of giving precisely the opposite testimony to
that which one would expect from him. I shall,
therefore, take the liberty of calling another witness, whose opinion I know in advance, and whose
expertness in these matters will be questioned by
no one. It is Mr. Henry James. In the lecture on
Balzac which Mr. James delivered from many
platforms in this country in 1905, occurs this
passage:

I do not propose for a moment to invite you to blink
the fact that our huge Anglo-Saxon array of producers
and readers — and especially our vast cis-Atlantic
multitude — presents production uncontrolled, production untouched by criticism, unguided, unlighted,
uninstructed, unashamed, on a scale that is really a

179

new thing in the world. It is the complete reversal of any proportion, between the elements, that was ever seen before. It is the biggest flock straying without shepherds, making its music without a sight of the classic crook, be-ribboned or other, without a sound of the sheep-dog's bark — wholesome note, once in a way — that has ever found room for pasture."

One may retort, of course, that Mr. James was himself a critic, and a critic with extraordinary powers of expression, or he could not have written that passage. True enough, but yet how lonely and bewildered is this cleverest of sheep-dogs as he wheels and barks in his immitigable predicament of endeavoring to guide the unguidable! If the flock be at the moment unmanageable, the very presence of a Poe or a James may add confusion and irritation to the collective mind of the sheep — so that even the most unbiased of observers may be tempted to say that the sheep-dogs might as well not be there at all, or, in less metaphorical terms, to assert that the literary man in this country has no critic.

But let us waive the argument from expert testimony, interesting as the witnesses may be. The everyday experience of men who read books and write books, of men who read American newspapers and magazines and write for American newspapers and magazines, is sufficiently conclu-

sive for our purpose. We all agree that the status
of literary criticism in America is unsatisfactory.
Those of us who write books assert that it is only
now and then, and by lucky accident, that our
books are competently reviewed. We get praise
enough, and sometimes blame enough — or nearly
enough — but we do not often get real criticism.
The reader and would-be buyer of books has
great difficulty in discovering what new books are
worth buying or reading. A generation ago one
could often depend upon the local bookseller for
this information, but, for well-known economic
reasons, the old type of bookseller has in most
towns been driven from business, and the young
lady who arranges her hair behind the book-
counter of the department store is obviously
puzzled by your questions. If you turn to the
newspapers for information about the twelve or
thirteen thousand books published in this country
every year, you find, it is true, a heroically com-
piled mass of book notices — many of them composed, in their essential features, by the advertising clerks of the publishers who are trying to sell
the books. There were never so many Saturday
and Sunday literary supplements and other guides
to the book-buyer; but there was never, even in the
eighteen-thirties, any less actual criticism in proportion to the number of books published. Here

and there, there is a daily or weekly journal that
endeavors, according to its abilities, to uphold
and to apply critical standards. I need not name
them, for they are rare enough to be generally
known. Technical treatises, it is true, frequently
meet with competent criticism in technical journals; although I have heard the editor of a scientific paper boast that he had dictated, in sixty
minutes, reviews of eleven new scientific books,
not one of which he had taken the trouble to read
beyond the preface and the table of contents. It
may be remembered that poor Poe, who had no
stenographer, thought that "the analysis of a
book is a matter of time and of mental exertion."

But technical treatises, and books written by
scholars for scholars, are not what I have in mind
in discussing the adequacy or inadequacy of current criticism. I have in mind what we call, by
common consent, books of general literature, the
literature to which a writing man, if he has any
ambition, hopes sooner or later to make a genuine
contribution. If literary men, as I believe they
do, and if readers of literature, as I am sure they
do, feel that American criticism is inadequately
equipped, that it is imperfectly performing its
task, and that its authority is but slightly re-
spected, the reasons must be traced in some deep-
lying conditions of the public mind.

III

WHAT is criticism, after all, and what has the public mind to do with it? We talk glibly in our academic classrooms about various types of literary criticism, the "judicial," the "interpretative," the "appreciative," the "impressionistic," and so forth. It is evident that these types or species of criticism exist and co-exist; that they are found not merely in the periodical literature of our own country and of all civilized countries, but that the processes indicated by the words "judicial," "interpretative," "impressionistic," may be traced not only in the work of any one critic, but even in successive pages of the same critical essay. As I have said elsewhere: "Some of the famous impressionists, like Lamb, Stevenson, Lemaître, and Anatole France, know a great deal more about the 'canons' than they wish at the moment to confess. They play so skillfully with the overtones of criticism because they know the fundamental tones so well. Stevenson attempts 'scientific' criticism in his essay on style, 'historical' criticism in his essay on Pepys. Jeffrey occasionally writes 'national character' criticism quite in the expository method of Sainte-Beuve. Coleridge and Emerson, Arnold and Ruskin, are too many-sided and richly endowed men to limit

their literary essays to any one type of criticism."
Necessary as it is, no doubt, to distinguish between the various species of criticism, and however great becomes the relative significance of one
type or another as we regard this or that historic
period or this or that individual practitioner of the
art of criticism, it ought surely to be possible to
reduce these varieties to the terms of a single process, to conceive of criticism as the performance
of a single act. I venture to call it, as it has often,
no doubt, been called before, the act of weighing.

I buy, for example, a pound of butter at the
grocer's. The grocer puts into one end of his
scales a piece of metal — whose exactness of
weight, one may add, is guaranteed by the State
— and into the pan at the other end of his scales
he drops a lump of butter, whose purity, as it
happens, is also guaranteed by the State. With a
practiced and, I trust, a dispassionate eye he
watches the indicator, adds to or subtracts from
the lump of butter until the scales declare that
the lump weighs precisely one pound, and with
that declaration the critical part of the transac-
tion is over. The grocer becomes again a friend,
a politician, a philosopher — perhaps a creditor;
he ceases to be a critic.

To this humble illustration of the function of
criticism there will be prompt and vigorous denial.

First, as to the analogy of the standard weight. There is no such thing as a standard weight in literature, cry many voices in chorus. That is the old Renaissance folly of measuring every new book by Homer or by Virgil. There is no such thing as any standard, recognized *"semper, ubique et ab omnibus."* That conception is passing with the very language in which your hackneyed quotation is dressed. Charles Lamb was fooling us when he attempted to distinguish between books that were books and books that were no-books — "a-biblia." To talk of a certain "fineness," as of gold, or a certain proportion, as in architecture, or a certain "mass" requisite for impression, as did Aristotle, is to hark back to the old nonsense about the "unities" and the "rules," about "decorum" and the "touchstones."

And even if there were a standard weight, cry other voices, there are no standard scales: no universal or general mind which is to be impressed by a particular piece of literature, which receives and records its impact. The modern doctrine of the relativity of knowledge and of taste has annihilated that conception. You can record the penetration of a projectile into steel or sandbags of a certain density, but there is no "general heart of man" which attests the impression made upon it by a poem or a play. We admit, it is true, that many persons of many races may have enjoyed this poem or this play; but to talk of measurements, of great, greater, and greatest poets and dramatists is absurd.

And then your "weigher!" continues the chorus of dissent. Even if there were ponderable weights and universally accepted scales, how is it possible that any one man should be expert in handling them; at once familiar with the properties and qualities of literature and with the modes of literary expression, infinitely undulating and various as these things must be? What impossible eyesight you demand of him! What delicacy! What detachment! What probity! What communicative skill is needed in reporting his results, in recording his literary judgments! No man can be trusted to weigh a book as he would weigh a lump of butter. Think of Jeffrey and his unlucky "This will never do!" The only criticism for our modern world is "creative" criticism, the adventures of one's own soul in the presence of masterpieces, the translation of sensations and emotions originating in books into exquisite new symbols "borrowed from all the other arts and from the inexhaustible stores of natural beauty." Abandon this wretched mechanism of your grocer's shop! Has not Professor Spingarn, surely an acute and accomplished student of the history of literary opinion, asserted in his "New Criticism" that "we have done with all the old rules," "we have done with the *genres*," "we have done with the comic, the tragic, the sublime," "we have done with the theory of style," "we have done with all moral judgment of literature," "with the race, the time, the environment," and "with the 'evolution' of literature": that, in short, we have now reached a moment when æsthetic judgment is identified with creative art, and "in their flashes of insight taste and genius are one"?

To these confident assertions of the New Criticism, I reply that "we have done" nothing of the sort. Around many an excited table in bohemian restaurants you can listen to enthusiastic repeals of the Ten Commandments, but in the prosaic light of the following morning "the Ten Commandments will not budge." You can attend delightful mass meetings where it is unanimously resolved that there shall be no more biological differences between the sexes — and then you can think it over on your way home. The answer to these facile generalizations of the New Criticism is to be found not in other generalizations, but in the history of book publication and in the facts of contemporary journalism. Books are produced, like any other economic product, in response to a demand. They are sold to the public, and the public insists, with varying degrees of urgency, on knowing, more or less accurately, what it is buying. You will observe that I am returning obstinately to the grocer's shop. There are some two hundred and fifty thousand grocers in the United States, and all of them, on this very day, have been weighing their butter. I do not assert that this process is equally honest or skillful in all the shops: indeed, it is upon this very variety with which the essential process is conducted that we find the closest analogy with the varieties of literary criticism. I am aware that in spite of State inspection there is some variation in the grocers' weights and in the mechanism of their scales; that there are garrulous grocers who talk when they should be weighing, philosophical grocers who have theories of their business, self-opinionated grocers who declare that they can tell a pound of butter by the eye or by the "heft" as accurately as if they weighed it. And upon the staffs of the twenty-five thousand American journals—dailies, weeklies, monthlies, and quarterlies—which attempt to weigh the merits of the twelve or thirteen thousand new books of each year, there are likewise garrulous and philosophical and self-opinionated reviewers: "indolent reviewers" and overworked reviewers, reviewers trained and untrained, one-eyed and blind. I am not asserting, of course, that the performance of the act of literary criticism and the specific task of reviewing new books are always identical; but it is fair to assume, as I have already assumed, that, if criticism is functioning in any country, the periodical journalism of that country instantly reflects its spirit, partakes of its vitality. And, conversely, when the tone of criticism is uncertain and feeble, journalism will betray this general debility of judgment.

While we may grant, then, that the present status of literary criticism in American periodicals is unsatisfactory, we have no warrant in saying that the act of judgment upon books and the art or trade of recording these judgments is disappearing. One has only to count the columns of "book talk" that are printed. Nor are we justified in maintaining that "we have done" with this or that specific type of criticism. Any one who keeps in touch with current journalism here — to say nothing of England or the Continent — becomes aware of the extraordinary eclecticism of contemporary criticism. Its practitioners still employ, perhaps under new names, every method of critical judgment and record which has ever proved its effectiveness. There is less, no doubt, of "magisterial" criticism than there used to be.

Critics do not risk so many "speeches from the throne" as formerly, fearing, perhaps, adverse parliamentary majorities. They do not quote Aristotle and Horace, Dacier and Addison with quite the old assurance. They may believe with Burke that there are times when we must abrogate our own rules in favor of our own principles, and that those times occur rather frequently. But even the New Mathematics, which has changed the rules for working out certain problems, allows, I believe, that for all practical purposes two and two still make four. What Poe called the "determinate principles" of criticism may still be regarded as the fundamental tone of which the "rules" are the shifting, hovering overtones.

Have we done with the study of the *genres?* I should say that the success of series of books like the "Channels of English Literature" or the "Types of English Literature" prove how fertile and stimulating a field for criticism was opened a score of years ago by the talent of Brunetière. Have we done, in our daily journalism even, with discussing the race, the time, the environment? By no means, though we may choose to alter the somewhat over-rigid lines drawn by Taine, or refuse to accept the theory of literary "evolution" in the precise terms laid down by Brunetière. Biologists, for that matter, do not now appear to

regard Darwin's "Origin of Species" as if that
epoch-making book were tables of a law graven
upon stone. Have we really done with the comic
and the tragic? Bergson's book on "Laughter"
set us all to fresh thinking on that perennial
topic, only the other day. Have we done "with all
moral judgment of literature"? Surely no one
can say that who has listened to women discussing
the latest magazine stories, or the comments of
men as they come out from the latest plays.
Newspaper reviewers are listeners; that is a part
of their function; and moral judgments of literature are forced in our day upon the most reluctant
minds — minds predisposed to assess literature
and art by æsthetic standards only. Until the
State no longer finds it necessary to say: "This
book shall not circulate in the mails," or, "this
play is too indecent to be acted," I do not see how
the literary critic can shrug his shoulders and say
that moral considerations are no part of his affair.
In so far as he is a good journalist, at any rate, he
must make it his affair; and I question whether
attention to "rules" and "*genres*" and "style"
and the "comic and the tragic" and "morals"
will prevent him in the least from experiencing
what Professor Spingarn has called those flashes
of insight in which taste and genius are one. It is
true that we can hardly expect to count upon

purchasing these flashes in every morning paper. We are lucky to get a glimpse of them in the "Atlantic" and "Yale Review."

The difficulty does not lie, then, in the amount or range of the critical writing in our American periodicals. Considering how little attention the book notices receive and how little authority they seem to exercise, it is surprising that they occupy as much space as they do. The mind of the journal-reading American public is at present indifferent to many if not to most of the questions raised by literary criticism. Whatever indictment is to be drawn against our periodical criticism lies fairly against the whole nation and not merely or primarily against the book-reviewing class of writing men. These reviewers are not, for the most part, well trained; but it is only recently that we are beginning to look at journalism as one of the real professions, to be prepared for like another. The reviewers are inadequately paid; and when we are tempted to find fault with their slovenly writing, we should remember what President Patton of Princeton once remarked when an instructor in the School of Science was accused of using ungrammatical English in the classroom: "It is hard to get Matthew Arnolds for twelve hundred dollars a year." The real difficulty is that these untrained and underpaid journalists are producing copy, as best they can, for a public which is genuinely interested in stock-market criticism, in baseball criticism, in political, social, and economic criticism, and, in a few cities, in musical and dramatic criticism, but which is not very eagerly interested in the criticism of books. To put it concretely, the "financial" page of a New York, Chicago, or Boston newspaper is likely to be more expertly edited and more expertly read than the "literary" page. It represents better journalism. It responds more immediately to the laws of demand and supply.

IV

AFTER all, what kinds or classes of persons are interested in periodical criticism? If we can succeed in visualizing these classes of persons, we shall see more clearly the obstacles to ideal literary criticism in American periodicals, and we shall find, I believe, that some of these obstacles are surmountable.

I adopt, for convenience, a serviceable classification made a few years ago by Mr. Charles Miner Thompson, an American working journalist, and a critic of rare courage and distinction. In an article entitled "Honest Literary Criticism" in the "Atlantic Monthly," for July, 1908, Mr. Thompson begins by saying: "There are five

groups interested in literary criticism: publishers
of books, authors, publishers of reviews, critics,
and, finally, the reading public." No one can
quarrel with this grouping, although the more
superstitious among us may be inclined to assert
that there is a sixth person present: namely,
Literature herself, the goddess whom we igno-
rantly worship, the divinity for whom a Poe or a
Sainte-Beuve will battle as other men fight for a
mistress or a flag. Men of letters, "the strangest
regiment in Her Majesty's service," as Thackeray
called them, have surely not lost, in our day, all of
their loyalty to the colors; and there are plenty of
ragged veterans and raw recruits who still salute
Literature, winning or losing, with the reverence
with which Frenchmen of the eighteen-thirties
saluted "Art." But we are looking for the moment at the day's work of the literary journalist,
and not at his silent loyalties. Let us keep to the
five groups.

"All five," says Mr. Thompson, "are discon-
tented with the present condition of American
criticism. Publishers of books complain that reviews do not help sales. Publishers of magazines
lament that readers do not care for articles on
literary subjects. Publishers of newspapers frankly
doubt the interest of book notices. The critic confesses that his occupation is ill-considered and ill-

paid. The author wrathfully exclaims — but what he exclaims cannot be summarized, so various is it. Thus, the whole commercial interest is unsatisfied. The public, on the other hand, finds book reviews of little service, and reads them, if at all, with indifference, with distrust, or with exasperation. That portion of the public which appreciates criticism as an art maintains an eloquent silence and reads French."

There is, of course, no single adequate explanation of this complicated series of facts, but Mr. Thompson thinks that the chief trouble is that our American criticism is not marked by intellectual candor. The publisher wishes his books praised, the publisher's advertising matter keeps the book-review publisher alive, and his money, in turn, supports the critic. Hence the Silent Bargain, and its result, disingenuous criticism. I cannot give here the details of Mr. Thompson's arraignment of the present system. Every practical journalist will, I think, agree with him in condemning the use of "ready-made notices, the perfunctory and insincere work of some minor employee" in the publisher's office; "the sending out, as 'literary' notes, of thinly disguised advertisements and irrelevant personalities." What does it signify to you or to me or to Literature, that two tons of paper are to be used in printing the advance orders of "G. G.'s Ears," or that the author of the "Outside of the Platter" has now read his last galley of proof and gone tarpon fishing? And yet the "publisher's notes" sent out by the foremost American houses are largely made up of such material as that. The curse of our so-called literary journalism is its complaisance, its social, intellectual, and commercial timidity. Watch its consequences in the "reading notice" of new books.

The inventor of the American "reading notice" is thought to be the late Mr. Azariah Smith, of Boston, a high-minded gentleman who selected from the advance sheets of the season's books published by his employers such passages and qualities as he could honestly praise. He had extraordinary deftness and tact, and when he could not praise, he was silent. But he produced, without knowing it, an instrument demoralizing to the conscience and the critical sense. Everybody who knows the inside of a publisher's office has seen this instrument at work. Here is a clever boy, often college-bred, at his desk in the publicity department. Under the direction of the publicity manager, he prepares "reading notices" or "literary notes" of the books shortly to be published by his employer. It is physically impossible for him to read all of these books. Very likely he has read none of them. But he has access to the reports of the manuscript readers, to the advance instructions prepared for the traveling salesmen, and he knows, from the advertising department, which books are to be "played up" as features of the coming campaign. And now he must "play up," too, or cease to hold his job; and he proceeds to compose reading notices about the new book and its author. He regards the book, quite naturally, as a commercial product which his house is trying to sell; it has cost hard money to manufacture it; it will cost some more money to advertise it; and it is his business to push the sale. Is the copy produced under such circumstances by the clever boy or the indurated veteran likely to be characterized by intellectual candor? Yet something like half or two thirds of the "book-talk" columns of most American newspapers are made up from paragraphs prepared in this fashion by the publishers themselves. "For my part," says the bookseller to Parson Adams in "Joseph Andrews," "the copy that sells best will be always the best copy in my opinion." Precisely. That book of human nature of which Fielding was the faithful historian has gone through many editions since the eighteenth century, but it is still being printed from the old plates. Publishers will be publishers.

Is the book-advertising in American periodicals
characterized by intellectual candor? The advertising of a book is a legitimate commercial venture, undertaken with the hope of a return. The
publisher selects from his prospective list of books
the probable leader or leaders: that is to say, the
books whose sales are most likely to respond to
advertising efforts. Some books, of course, cannot be sold with any amount of advertising, and
some can be sold without any advertising at all;
and between these extremes lies the debatable
land. The publisher debates, decides, and puts
his money on certain authors. In the language of
the race-track, he "plays the favorites" unless he
has a gambler's faith in his dark horses; perhaps
he plays both. His advertising clerks instantly
reflect the employer's faith or lack of faith in
certain books; the advertising copy prepared for
the newspapers and magazines is an accurate in-
dication of the relative cash value of the authors
upon the publisher's list, as the season begins. As
the season advances, these values change, precisely like the positions of horses in a race. The
shrewdest publisher may find that he has put his
money on the wrong horse, and then follows a
tardy revision of advertising copy, a new distribu-
tion of adjectives and adverbs of praise. I am not
blaming the publisher for the system under which

he is forced, or at least honestly believes himself forced, to do business; but I ask where in all these millions of pages of advertising matter are we to expect intellectual candor?

The courts have something to say about the advertising of patent medicines. They insist that the label shall indicate the contents of the bottle. We have no pure-food law for magazines or books. And no one dreams of advocating such a law, not even in the present craze for law-making. Misleading advertising of books must be left to defeat itself, as it ultimately will. But in the mean time it produces widespread demoralization of the critical sense, and creates an atmosphere highly unfavorable to accuracy of judgment and honesty of record.

v

LET us now consider the actual reviewer of new books. Who is he? What are the chances of his possessing the intellectual candor which should characterize all reviewing? And if he does possess it, what are the conditions under which he may say what he really thinks? Mr. Charles Miner Thompson, who has himself passed through the successive phases of experience of a newspaper reviewer, of editor and publisher, does not draw a flattering picture of the persons who actually write the reviews: "Commonly in the newspapers and frequently in periodicals of some literary pretension, the writers of reviews are shiftless literary hacks, shallow, sentimental women, or crude young persons full of indiscriminate enthusiasm for all printed matter." True enough, no doubt, and yet there are hundreds of reviewers of a better sort, college-trained young men and young women who have some notion of literary standards, plenty of professional ambition, a tolerable skill in writing, and who would really like to do their best. What happens when the new book is assigned to one of them? The book has been preceded or accompanied, it will be remembered, by the publisher's reading notice of it, which lies there upon your desk, next to the scissors and paste-pot. Often the "literary note" is in the form of a ready-made review, couched in the language of the man who is trying indirectly to sell the book. It is well written — better written, in four cases out of five, than your own notice would be. And there also is the advertisement of the book, written by the man who is directly trying to sell it. Neither one of these men is thinking or writing with the mind of a critic; both are using very naturally the psychology and the vocabulary of the promoter. Will the boy at the reviewer's desk have the intellectual candor and the power of will to see the book as it is, rather than as the publisher would like him to see it? Can he and will he "weigh" the book and report his verdict?

Fortunately for the honor of American journalism, the young reviewer often says his honest say, and so does many an older reviewer. And not all publishers and advertisers are disingenuous, and there are hundreds of books in every spring and fall season which deserve the praise they receive. But no man can grow from a young reviewer into an old one without coming into prompt and humiliating contact with that system of control which the advertiser of books tends to exercise over the literary columns of the periodicals which print his advertising matter and review his books. This system is extremely simple. Copies of all reviews are sent to the publisher: if these reviews tend to be unfavorable, the publisher will often cut down or threaten to cut down his advertising; and then the counting-room of the newspaper wants to know why the young reviewer cannot take a more "reasonable" attitude of mind. That is all: and if the reviewer's living is dependent upon his taking a "reasonable" view, he often surrenders. The Silent Bargain has been struck. The reviewer does what is expected of him, and he will find some day that his epitaph has already been written for him by Oliver Goldsmith:

"Here lies poor Ned Purdon, from misery freed,
    Who long was a bookseller's hack.
He led such a damnable life in this world,
    I don't think he'll wish to come back."

I am not, of course, putting a theoretical case.
Any publisher's office or newspaper office has its
own stories to tell. In fact, since I began to write
these pages, I have stopped to listen to the adventures of a young newspaper man, a recent graduate
of that joyous school of journalism, the Harvard
"Lampoon," who is now doing the literary and
dramatic criticism for an evening paper in an
inland city. This boy's amazed discovery that his
light-hearted notices of certain very light fiction
brought rebuking response from the publishers,
from the manager of the local bookstore, and from
the counting-room, was comic, and it would have
been tragic if the "Lampoon" humorist had not
demonstrated in other ways his value to his newspaper. But he does not joke any more about the
advertisers: he has seen, in a flash of illumination,
the relation between the far-away publishers and
the weekly pay-envelope of the cub reviewer.

Our country exhibits almost every conceivable
gradation of literary criticism. We must avoid
easy generalizations about it. But looking at it
broadly, and in the light of foreign periodical
criticism, it lacks candor, it lacks trained intelli-

gence, and it lacks distinction. Most of the book notices prepared by the newspapers themselves are written hastily by staff writers, who are overworked, underpaid, and to whom questions of literary criticism are not matters of the first importance. A great many of the solid and brilliant literary contributions to foreign newspapers are written outside of the office. If we find German criticism more competent than ours, Italian criticism more vigorous, French criticism more artistic, English criticism more indefinably bookish, we must remember that we are judging this criticism by its best examples, and that these examples are the work of professional critics. Our book-reviewing is often ambitious enough, but it reveals the limitations of the amateur.

VI

A GOOD working illustration of the qualities and defects of our book-reviewing can easily be found by any one who is willing to study the press clippings about any representative book. The press bureaus clip industriously, and every publisher keeps on file as complete a collection of clippings as he can secure. Let us look at one of these collections. It should be remembered that no publisher can afford to send a copy of each of his new books to more than a limited number of newspapers. If he sends out a hundred press copies of a serious book he thinks he is spending a good deal of money, and the occasions when he sends out over two or three hundred press copies of even a presumably popular book are very rare indeed. Remember likewise that the newspaper assumes no obligation to review the books sent to it; although it is aware that, if it neglects flagrantly to notice its press copies, it will soon lose its place upon the complimentary list. Ordinarily, then, the collection of clippings will show that each press copy has elicited some sort of notice, perfunctory or otherwise. As a matter of fact, something like one-half of the clippings gathered by the bureaus are mere reproductions, with minor variations, of the "literary note" or "ready-made review" originally furnished by the publisher himself. One half, then, of the clippings, are negligible for our purpose, though highly useful to the publisher in spreading broadcast what is called a "sympathetic" attitude toward the book.

As one turns over the significant half, he is struck by the fact that outside of a score of leading newspapers the most vivacious and penetrating comments have often been made in obscure journals — often in the book columns of some sectarian religious paper, or in a remote country weekly whose staff happens to include a man or woman of some leisure, pungency, originality, freshness of mental attitude. Sometimes these contributors are very young — like my friend of the "Lampoon" — and they drift in time to the great cosmopolitan newspapers, where they are likely to have other and supposedly more important assignments than book-reviewing. It is interesting, at any rate, to find in a bundle of clippings fresh evidence that the real mental life of this country is not to be judged by its so-called "cosmopolitan" journalism; that throughout the United States there are plenty of unregarded persons who can think straight and write with candor. Such persons will count in the future evolution of American criticism.

But let us come back to a specific bundle of press clippings. I have asked permission to examine all the reviews of "The Letters of Charles Eliot Norton" — surely one of the notable issues of the last publishing season. The two volumes were most attractive in form, and were admirably edited. Mr. Norton was not a figure of primary significance in literature, but throughout a long life he enjoyed a peculiar intimacy with primary men — with Carlyle, Emerson, Ruskin, and many others. He sums up a whole generation of New England academic culture. He was himself a most interesting, lovable, many-sided person, full of gayety and of melancholy and of passionate patriotism. Now what did American periodicals have to say about the story of his life and friendships?

The answer can be given briefly: they said almost nothing that was really illuminating in matter, or that showed delicacy or distinction of style. Setting aside Mr. Howells's reminiscent article in the "North American Review," which was a well-nigh perfect example of what a literary portrait may be, the three best reviews, in my judgment, were not American at all. They appeared in the London "Athenæum," "Times," and "Nation." Why these English articles were better written than the American articles I cannot endeavor to explain. The three next best reviews were printed in the New York "Sun," the New York "Times," and the New York "Nation": there were respectably good articles in a few other newspapers, and the remainder of the big bundle was negligible. Of course, the press-clipping bureau may have failed to collect all the reviews. The books were expensive, and it is likely that few press copies went to those local or "class" journals which often publish, as I have said, surprisingly good notices. I may have failed in my assessment of relative values. But making allowance for a wide margin of such errors, I do not think my verdict upon the total value of that collection of clippings can be set aside.

In further pursuit of perfectly concrete evidence, I have examined the press notices of a notable series of books, namely, the Journals of Emerson. Here there can be no question as to the distinction and the significance of the author: Emerson, surely, belongs at the high table. Nine volumes of his Journals have appeared at intervals since 1909, under the competent editorship of Emerson's son and grandson; and the tenth and final volume has just been issued. The critical reviews in France began to publish articles on these Journals five years ago. What have our American periodicals had to say? Among the hundreds of clippings collected, there is everywhere evidence of quick intelligence and of journalistic knack in presenting salient aspects of the highly miscellaneous matter contained in the Journals. The better American criticisms were, in this instance, fully equal and I think superior to the English notices;— the English reviewers seeming to understand their Norton better than their Emerson. The newspapers printed in American cities of secondary importance, like Indianapolis, Louisville, Newark, Springfield, gave more space to the Journals than the newspapers of Chicago or Philadelphia; indeed, I should say that the successive volumes were more adequately reviewed in the Indianapolis "News" than in any other paper except the New York "Sun." The newspaper criticisms, furthermore, were distinctly better — with perhaps one exception — than the comments of the professedly "literary" weeklies and monthlies. But nowhere in this country, as far as I have been able to discover, has there yet appeared a really noteworthy, not to say epoch-making article, upon these richly suggestive Journals of one of our foremost men; nothing which would be memorable either to the student of Emerson or to the lover of literature. It is inconceivable that English or Continental literary periodicals would not have given more attention to the posthumously published work of one of their own national writers of Emerson's rank.

VII

THE mention of Norton and of Emerson suggests another curious lack in our contemporary criticism, the absence, namely, of that kind of literary portrait which Mr. Howells drew of Mr. Norton and of Mark Twain, and which he had drawn before in his masterly volume entitled "My Literary Friends and Acquaintances." The expertness of Mr. Henry James in this field of concrete criticism needs no testimony. But after we have mentioned these two artists, who is left?[1] Think what a portrait of Norton Sainte-Beuve would have painted, after his devouring eyes had run through the two volumes of the "Letters"! What charm and color there is in Howells's picture of Cambridge in the eighteen-sixties and eighteen-seventies!

But there is charm and color in the newer Cambridge too; or rather there was, only the other day! Why has no one painted it? There was Shaler, who wrote the early chapters of his autobiography with the concreteness of a Defoe, the grace of a Le Sage. He was known by thousands of Harvard men: he was an intimate of many scientists and men of letters: he has been dead only eight years, yet he is already the shadow of a shade. No one has really drawn him in any of his characteristic poses; no one has pictured his insight and his vanity, his flashing brilliancy and his human charm. There was Shaler's friend, William James. His books are read by scholars and pupils all over the world. But who will record the vibration of his rich baritone voice, his shyness, his whimsicality, his kindness, the strain of the irresponsible Irishman in him? Or take, finally, one

[1] This passage was written before the publication of the series of admirable literary portraits by Gamaliel Bradford.

other Cambridge personage, John Fiske, with his huge body, big brain, and big heart. Who dares render the actual breathing, hungry, and thirsty animal of him, and his Rabelaisian laughter, his follies, his sentimentality, his intellectual and commercial makeshifts: in short, the whole lovable weakness and strength of that great boy! John Fiske was as real as Boswell's Johnson and in another ten years he will be as remote as Jared Sparks.

We are not only afraid of the literary portrait, but we also shrink, even in our professedly literary periodicals, from serious critical studies of living fellow countrymen. Mr. W. C. Brownell's "Atlantic" article on Henry James is almost the sole instance I can now recall, in recent years, of a really trenchant and exhaustive analysis of the artistic powers of a living American writer. When Stedman's notable series of papers on the Poets of America was printed in the "Century Magazine," Whittier and Holmes, Lowell and Whitman were, it is true, still living, although their characteristic work had long been done. But if we will examine the careful bibliography of critical articles upon these writers in Professor Page's "Chief American Poets," we shall become aware that very few of the more significant critiques appeared during the productive years of the poets in question. Thomas Bailey Aldrich never lived,

I think, to see any adequate review and assessment of his work, and, indeed, it would have been a stout-hearted man of letters who would have risked incurring Aldrich's wrath. No such study as Mr. Charlton Lewis has recently made of William Vaughn Moody's verse appeared during Moody's lifetime. I remember that the "Revue des deux Mondes," a half-dozen years ago, printed a twenty-page criticism of the work of Henry van Dyke. If any American periodical has attempted a similarly serious and exhaustive analysis of the work of this talented and popular writer, I am unaware of it. There are publisher's notes about such men, by the thousand; there are agreeable little articles written by their personal friends or nasty little articles composed by their enemies; but there is no criticism. This is surely what Emerson meant by saying in 1836 that "the literary man in this country has no critic"; that a writer can grow from youth to maturity, and make his professional way and sell his books by the hundred thousand, and yet never see, for his guidance or comfort or chastisement, from the beginning to the end of his literary career, a single competent and authoritative critical verdict upon his work — such verdicts as would be his by right if he were publishing books in England, France, Germany, or Russia.

CRITICISM IN AMERICAN PERIODICALS

The curious element in our American situation is this divorce between the judgments of private conversation and the conventional banalities of the published literary column. Go to a club or a dinner party and ask the first man or woman you meet for a private opinion of the books of Henry van Dyke, of Hopkinson Smith, of Winston Churchill, of Mrs. Wharton; and you will get an answer, for the work of these writers has not been done in a corner. The answer will often be admirable in its succinctness, its poise, its temper, and phrasing; in short, in its expression of the spirit of true criticism. But the path from private talk to public utterance is marked with a "No thoroughfare."

One explanation has been sought in the fact that most of our literary journals have been the property and in some sense the organs of great publishing houses. These houses have not welcomed the frank criticism of their own authors, believing that such criticisms might affect adversely the sales of their books; and through considerations of trade courtesy, the influence of the owners of literary journals has been thrown against the frank criticism of other authors whose books appear upon the trade list of their rivals. This reciprocal abnegation of the rights of criticism has no doubt existed; and unquestionably the

ownership of a critical journal by a publishing
house is highly undesirable, in the interests of a
free and impartial criticism. But I think that a
more obvious explanation is to be found in a kind
of social self-consciousness which is typically
American. One of the old members of the Boston
Saturday Club — I think it was Dr. Holmes —
used to say that he cared more for what the members of the Club thought of his writings than for
what the public thought. No doubt he did, but it
may be questioned whether he always knew what
the other members of the Club were really thinking! Hawthorne and Emerson, for example, were
two well-known members of the Saturday Club.
Each recorded in his private diary his high opinion
of the other man; but each added, in effect, that
he thought his friend's books were empty and
unreadable. If either of them had elaborated his
private opinion in print, the luncheons of the
Club thereafter might have lost something of their
charm. The fact is, that, unless we are natural
Ishmaelites like Sainte-Beuve and Poe, we have
often to choose, as Mr. C. M. Thompson has
said, between admirable conduct and admirable
criticism.

Thoroughgoing literary criticism of a contemporary is an extraordinarily delicate affair. Criticism of a composer by a musician, of a painter by

an art critic, or even such craftsman-criticism as Coleridge passed upon Wordsworth, or Poe upon Bryant and Longfellow, is relatively objective and dispassionate, compared with the total verdict upon a contemporary writer's mind and heart. Even in France, where there is a freer social tradition, and where intellectual causes far outweigh any personal considerations, the social and personal obstacles to full critical freedom have been felt. But if France and Russia and Germany are occasionally too bold in these matters for the finest scrupulosity of conduct, we are certainly too timid. We take our mental notes, no doubt, but we dare not print them.

This timidity, which is partly social and partly commercial, is accentuated by a widespread feeling among potential critics that it would make little difference whether they spoke out or not. They believe that few persons would be really interested. Mr. Thompson, from whose plea for honest literary criticism I have already quoted so often, is confident that many persons would be interested. Once establish a reign of candor, he believes, and critical journals would flourish. The whole intellectual atmosphere would be cleared and stimulated, publishers would cease their puffing, their disingenuous advertising, and would sell more books than they sell now. The example of Germany seems pertinent. There, at least, is a criticism far more untrammeled and candid than ours; and there is a book-trade established on more solid foundations. Without the American methods of securing publicity, a serious book published in Germany has a larger market than it commands here. The American circulation of a substantial contribution to general literature — say in the field of biography, history, essays, poetry — is, as all publishers know to their sorrow, extremely limited. A sale of twenty-five hundred copies is a respectable success; one of four thousand copies a solid success; anything beyond that is something to rub one's hands over. I have frequently asked publishers what they thought was the size of the possible American audience for a purely literary production, including fiction — that is to say, including novels which are read for their literary merits alone, as distinguished from the so-called "best sellers," which owe much of their circulation to the element of social imitation and literary fashion. Never but once have I heard a publisher estimate the possible audience for a purely literary production — that is, including all the persons who might be reached if the publisher knew how to reach them — as high as forty thousand. The more usual estimate is from ten to twenty thousand. The fact is, we are not a book-reading people. The vast majority of our ninety-odd millions of population have no literary appetites which cannot be supplied by the newspapers, the magazines, and an occasional "best-seller" novel. Whether the establishment of a reign of critical candor would materially alter these facts, one cannot say.

But I think it is indisputable that writers endowed with critical ability feel at present that there is but a slender demand for their services. They themselves, too often, show the general skepticism as to the validity, or what Professor Trent calls the "authority," of criticism. They are troubled by the old taunt that reviewers are men who have themselves failed; that no man would write criticism if the creative impulse were strong within him; that criticism remains, after all is said, a gray and sad second-best. I cannot stop to debate this old question, nor to attempt to apply to twentieth-century America the principles laid down in Arnold's classic essay on "The Function of Criticism at the Present Time." I content myself with saying that every kind of intellectual activity seems second-best to a second-best man, and that to a first-rate man there is no kind of intellectual activity which is not of first-rate importance.

VIII

IT is true that the past history and the actual present status of periodical criticism in this country show very clearly some of the obstacles which must be overcome before criticism touches directly the mind of the greater public. Its audience is limited, its practitioners are often half-hearted or imperfectly trained, publishers are skeptical, magazine editors are afraid, successful authors affect a contempt for it, the voice of honest criticism seems drowned in the din of commercial exploitation by the auctioneers and advertisers of the book of the afternoon, and, to put the worst charge last, "my people love to have it so." These obstacles are real, and they are not to be dismissed with a mere optimistic gesture. But are they fatal to the progress and the influence of genuine criticism? I cannot think so.

Take the fact of the limited audience. No matter how limited we think it is to-day, it was certainly more limited still in 1836, when Emerson declared that we had no critic, and Poe set himself doggedly, month after month, in the "Southern Literary Messenger," to demonstrate that there was at least one critic to be reckoned with. And how much this indefatigable advocate of the determinate principles of criticism accomplished at his lonely post! With better health, and better temper, and with that broader and deeper culture which was denied to him, what might not this theorist and craftsman have done for American criticism in spite of the small circle of subscribers to the "Messenger," and in spite of the indifference of the general public! The American critic of to-day who can enunciate a principle or record with delicacy and beauty and absolute honesty a critical verdict for a few thousand readers in the "Dial," the "Nation," the "Yale Review," need not worry about the limits of his audience. It is the small audience that is the vital, the responsive, the propagating audience. A friend of mine, years ago, made something of a reputation by means of brief book notices in "Life." They were clever, delicate, trenchant. He wanted — as we all want, at one time or another — the bigger audience: and he had his chance at it for six months by writing "book talk" in the pages of a certain publication which was then printing nine hundred thousand copies a month. My friend was radiant. "Think of it," he exclaimed, "my name will appear three times in each issue; once on the cover, and at the head and foot of each article. That means two million, seven hundred thousand repetitions of my little trade-mark, every month!" Six months later I

asked him how the trade-mark was working.
"Do you know," he said, "I never heard one
word from those articles, not one word!" He had
poured his witty sentences, drop by drop, into the
"unplumbed, salt, estranging sea" of prosperous
Philadelphia. Even granted that publicity is a
desirable ambition for a literary critic, as it
doubtless is, the way to attain unto it is to in-
struct your smaller circle. If that widens gradually, well and good, if it does not, you are still in
good company, and you can leave the Chautauqua
circuits of criticism to the publicists who adorn
them.

The obstacle to the popular influence of literary
criticism lies not so much in the real or supposed
limits of the audience, as in the half-heartedness
and the half-training of those of us who practice it.

> "It was never for the mean;
> It requireth courage stout."

Not merely the "two-o'clock-in-the-morning"
courage of the journalist who knows that the
paper must go to press and that his hastily pen-
ciled adjective must be, for that day at least, his
final adjective! The literary critic, like the musical and dramatic critic, needs sometimes that
courageous promptness and decision, but most of
his work is done under less pressing conditions of

time. His bravery must usually be that which asserts a well-considered opinion in the face of fashion and the mob. It is the "Athanasius-contra-mundum" courage; the courage which the present-day champions of Greek studies ought to show and do not always show; the courage of a solitary scholar like the late Professor Churton Collins, who declared that "Criticism is to literature what legislation and government are to states. If they are in able and honest hands, all goes well; if they are in weak and dishonest hands, all is anarchy and mischief."

It takes some courage in the scholar to assert the principles of the magistracy of criticism in a generation inclined to the doctrine of popular initiative, referendum, and recall: it takes far more courage in the journalist to apply judicial criticism to the season's books. To put on the black cap is no joking matter. An editor said once to Churton Collins: "If I were to tell the truth, as forcibly as I could wish to do, about the books sent to me for review, in six months my proprietors would be in the bankruptcy court." "It is in the power of the publishers," Collins added, "to ruin any literary journal. There is probably not a single review in London which would survive the withdrawal of the publishers' advertisements." The type of courage needed by the critic is not merely that temperamental obstinacy of which Churton Collins possessed, perhaps, more than his share; it is the intellectual courage which results from discipline, from breadth and sureness of knowledge. Before the critic can pronounce with any authority the wise and salutary verdict, "Thou ailest, here, and here," he must have had his professional training. He must know many languages and many literatures, many men of many minds, he must be in the current of ideas, he must be in touch with science and history and the organization of human society. We are quite willing to let a Goethe say, "This will never do," even though he happen to be wrong; we regard it as a casual mistake of a sound practitioner. We are irritated by the "This will never do" of a Francis Jeffrey, even though he happen to be entirely right, if we suspect that he is deficient in breadth of view, in fullness of knowledge, in richness of professional experience.

What is needed for our American periodical criticism is the enlistment in its service of more of these courageous and trained individuals. We have enough special organs of criticism; and the space devoted to criticism — or at least to book reviews and book talk — by our newspapers and magazines is certainly as ample as one could wish. The defects are those of quality, of competence, of real authority. How are these defects to be remedied? One proposal is that of the endowed newspaper, financially independent of the forces that militate against honest criticism. But a certain distrust attaches to all reforms which begin with "passing the hat." The arguments for a subsidized orchestra, a subsidized municipal theater or art museum, forceful as they are, are not quite convincing when applied to a newspaper or a magazine. The problem of better literary criticism must be worked out in journals with actual human subscribers and human advertisers, with real economic "persons" and in accordance with normal economic laws. Perhaps art cannot be trusted to make its way without a "patron" of some sort, individual or communal; but literature has gained immensely in emancipating itself first from the "patronage" of royalty and the nobility, and next from the patronage of the bookseller. It is only when the public has been the real patron of literature that the interests of literature have been secure. There is no evidence that the endowed newspaper or magazine would print better criticism than the privately owned newspaper or magazine would print if there were a public demand for it; and that the real public would be increased by endowed organs of criticism is extremely doubtful.

There are certain men whose contributions would be of great assistance to our critical journals, who chafe against the anonymous, unrecognized work of literary journalism. Nine tenths of the book-reviewing must probably continue to be turned out by staff writers, by desk-men who accept the conditions under which such work is to be done. You cannot hire young Brunetières for fifty or sixty dollars a week, but you can engage for that sum a steady-going hack-writer of fair intelligence and some experience, who is willing to forego the chance of personal prestige, and to find his satisfaction, as the best journalists find theirs, in working "for the paper," in the faith that their paper is serving the public. Such men have made the great refusal. They accept anonymity, as they accept the transiency of all periodical writing, as one of the conditions of the profession. Their heart's blood flows gayly into the melting-pot of "to-day's paper," and they are quite aware that the "life" of the signed magazine article or of the book is likely to be only a few days longer than the life of daily journalism. These desk-men, or, if you please, "hacks," will always do most of the critical weighing; and one of the main problems of periodical criticism is to increase their intelligence, their candor, and their professional pride.

I think it may fairly be said that our American

periodicals do not utilize all of the effective artillery of criticism that might be called into service. Every magazine editor has authoritative names upon his list of possible authors of critical articles. Sometimes he cannot afford to pay what the time and experience of such men is worth; more often he is convinced that the possible article would not bring a sufficiently tangible return to justify the space and the honorarium. Here is that fatal circle of distrust of the authority and influence of criticism, which coils itself around the minds of editors and the public. It is the old "What's the use?" It is the Mephistophelian "Geist der stets verneint." "What interest has Greenough to make a good statue?" writes Emerson in that same year, 1836, when he complained of our lack of literary criticism. "Who cares whether it is good? a few prosperous gentlemen and ladies; but the universal Yankee nation roaring in the Capitol to approve or condemn would make his eye and hand and heart go to a new tune." Yet nothing seems to me clearer than the necessity of breaking the fatal circle, and demonstrating that the public would have an interest in criticism if it could secure the criticism which is its right. If nine tenths of the work of periodical criticism must continue to be done by routine "desk-men," it is all the more necessary to enlist the services of the "tenth man." He must be well enough paid to make him independent of the malign influences which cripple the freedom and the candor of opinion. The work and the example of this tenth man would strengthen the professional courage and the self-respect of every anonymous book-reviewer.

"I want" — said Napoleon when he was founding the University of France — "a teaching body, because such a body never dies, but transmits its organization and its spirit. I want a body whose teaching is far above the fads of the moment, which goes straight on even when the government is asleep." No one has ever described in better terms than those the function of a great critical journal. I am not arguing for the prevalence of any one type of criticism in any given organ of critical opinion. It may be that at present our desirable tenth man in American periodical criticism should represent what is sometimes called "academic" criticism; that is, a respect for "the collective wisdom of the past," for the "more or less ascertainable degrees of value in the various *genres* of artistic production." Yet I agree with Professor Trent, from whom I quote these descriptions of academic criticism, in thinking that the impressionist critic is "the best critic for the new writers and hence for the majority of

227

contemporary readers." These scouts and report-
ers, as Mr. Trent calls them, perform a most
useful service to any periodical in discovering the
new men and the new literary methods. Those of
us whose minds are made up already, who love the
old practitioners, and who discourse garrulously
of old literary campaigns, would ruin any contemporary periodical if we had the exclusive direction
of its policy.

The ideal organ of literary criticism should
utilize every variety of training, of conviction,
and of what Fenimore Cooper called "gifts." It
should have its representatives of judicial, of
interpretative, and of purely impressionistic
criticism. Like the Church, it should employ
every variety of temperament, every range of
scholarship, every pattern of personal inventiveness and initiative, every mode of discipline, and
every mood of devotion. It should have its
Bishops and Archbishops for the various dioceses
of learning and of taste — perhaps its College of
Cardinals and its Pope, for there must always be
some Editor-in-Chief to keep the heretics in their
proper place; — but the essential thing is that it
should be a Church Militant, with daring young
missionaries and explorers, bent upon the con-
quest and conversion of the whole Philistine
world.

If the Mephistophelian doubter asks how a forward movement in criticism is possible in the face of the skepticism of publishers, the timidity of magazine editors, the contempt of commercially successful authors, and — worst of all — the tacit acceptance of these conditions by the public, I reply that a genuine forward movement of competent, candid, and militant criticism always creates its own public, establishes new conditions, and inevitably makes its way. The apparent preoccupation of the public with other issues is never a complete preoccupation. The public, like Nature herself, has a curious instinct for impassive waiting and watching until it sees what it wants. Musical criticism in this country has made a steady advance, always a little ahead of the musical education of the public, but constantly gaining in authority and courage as the standard of public appreciation of music has risen. The progress of architectural and art criticism has likewise corresponded to the development of public taste, always in advance of it, yet always being overtaken by it. Dramatic criticism has seemed to move in our day in a circle; the criticism of poetry and fiction seems just now to be retrograding as the public taste for poetry and fiction has grown less refined. But nobody supposes that the æsthetic education of a vast democracy like ours advances uniformly all along the line. The crucial question is whether your democracy is educatable. Academic persons believe that it is, or they would not be devoting their time to education. They have had to choose between John Stuart Mill and Carlyle, and they have taken their stand by the side of Mill. They hold that our democracy is capable of education, even of æsthetic education, and that an adequate sense of what is due to the public is the most essential equipment of the educator.

No one can watch the development of our current journalism without becoming aware that this sense of responsibility to the public is raising the whole level of the American press. The cub reporter learns to forget himself in serving his paper and his paper in turn gains in dignity and responsibility, in direct proportion to its consciousness of serving the interests of the public. It is in this hope that schools of journalism are founded, that dozens of universities, in the last five years, have undertaken courses dealing directly with journalistic work. But the standards taught in schools of journalism are already the working policies of the most influential American newspapers. And these standards of professional ethics, it should be remembered, have been maintained and clarified in the last fifteen years — a period most unfavor-

able to clear and quiet thinking, a period characterized rather by loose and excited thinking, by
floods of foaming talk, much of it debauching and
bedeviling to the puzzled private citizen; a period
characterized above all — if I may quote Emerson
for the last time — by "too much comment on the
movement by the mover."

If our journalism, under these circumstances of
ethical, social, economic, and political upset and
excitement — containing as they do, no doubt,
the seeds of many a future benefit — has made
steady gains in public spirit, in devotion to what it
considers to be the real interests of American
democracy, then we are warranted in believing
that the literary criticism of American periodicals
will gain in authority, in certainty of touch and
taste, by accepting the inflexible, the salutary
law of service to the public. It has served publishers, booksellers, and authors, with the results
that we have seen; it has voiced in turn the counting-room, the whim of the individual critic, the
tastes of the so-called literary class. Let it now
serve the public, without fear or favor, and it will
make sooner or later the astounding discovery
that the public is on its side.

THE END